Leadership Intelligence

Leadership Intelligence

Navigating to Your True North

Wanda Maulding Green
and Ed Leonard

ROWMAN & LITTLEFIELD
Lanham • Boulder • New York • London

Published by Rowman & Littlefield
A wholly owned subsidiary of The Rowman & Littlefield Publishing Group, Inc.
4501 Forbes Boulevard, Suite 200, Lanham, Maryland 20706
www.rowman.com

Unit A, Whitacre Mews, 26-34 Stannary Street, London SE11 4AB

British Library Cataloguing in Publication Information Available

Library of Congress Cataloging-in-Publication Data

Names: Maulding Green, Wanda, author. | Leonard, Edward, 1948- author.
Title: Leadership intelligence : navigating to your true north / Wanda Maulding Green and Edward Leonard.
Description: Lanham : Rowman & Littlefield, 2016.
Identifiers: LCCN 2016023483 (print) | LCCN 2016032737 (ebook) | ISBN 9781475827477 (cloth : alk. paper) | ISBN 9781475827484 (pbk. : alk. paper) | ISBN 9781475827491 (Electronic)
Subjects: LCSH: Leadership.
Classification: LCC BF637.L4 .M358 2016 (print) | LCC BF637.L4 (ebook) | DDC 158/.4–dc23
LC record available at https://lccn.loc.gov/2016023483

∞™ The paper used in this publication meets the minimum requirements of American National Standard for Information Sciences—Permanence of Paper for Printed Library Materials, ANSI/NISO Z39.48-1992.

Printed in the United States of America

Contents

Acknowledgments

We would surely be remiss not to take a moment to thank those who have had a hand in guiding us to the creation and culmination of this work. First, a sincere thank you to Tom Koerner at Rowman & Littlefield for giving us the opportunity to publish our ideas. A big shoutout goes to Bethany Janka for her responsiveness and attentiveness throughout the process.

A wealth of gratitude goes to my incredible husband, Steve, for his patience, support, encouragement, and unending sense of humor throughout this process; not only has he been helpful, but he has inspired my thinking in so many ways. Also, a genuine and heartfelt thanks to my mentor, colleague, and friend, Ed Leonard, who always, always, had belief in me and gently prodded me along to complete this work. Love and thanks to my sweet Southern mom for instilling many of the LSI competencies I continue to work on today, and finally, to my dad for his lifetime of *imprints*.

Ed would like to thank his beautiful wife, Mrs. L (Mrs. Carolyn Leonard) for her patience, support, encouragement, and technical assistance in helping with the preparation of the manuscript.

To you all, we are very grateful.

—*Wanda Maulding Green*

Preface

Over the last decade, based on experience and in conversations with former and current school principals, as well as professors of educational leadership, it has become evident that an extremely valuable component is missing in the training of school leaders. Training is needed in the area of soft skills, specifically those related to interpersonal relationships, communication dynamics, and group dynamics.

Interestingly, this need *crosses over* into many other disciplines as well. In a study in the business sector, for example, when senior management has a critical mass of 'soft skills,' their divisions outperformed other divisions by nearly 20 percent.[1] Furthermore, most colleges of medicine have personnel employed for the distinct purpose of training new physician interns in 'bedside' manner. Obviously, this is a skillset that not everyone is born with, and furthermore, we know and understand that leaders need this skillset and it may be learned.

Colleagues in leadership positions at all levels consistently share that the most challenging aspect of their job is managing people. Over and over former students entering leadership positions (as well as veteran administrators) say that the most challenging thing they have to do in their jobs is to have difficult conversations with other adults, singly or in groups. Moreover, the current literature is replete with discussions regarding not only the need for capable leaders but also for them to be well versed in the soft/people skills necessary to navigate the organizations they lead to success.

This book will examine five critical factors which undergird the tenets of Leadership Intelligence (LSI), through the lens of the soft skills of a leader, and why some leaders seem to have a 'greater intensity' of these factors than their peers. Furthermore, the following chapters will reveal how a leader can develop or enhance these skills, and how he/she can avoid leadership derailment, due to neglecting them. The book in totality is about the requisite soft skills that are foundational to *LSI* and how to master those skills.

From this perspective, we share a model (the Leadership GPS model) that identifies the personal strengths and weaknesses of leaders based on the five factors. Think about it. What could the CEO of an organization accomplish with a GPS for leadership—a tool with guiding advice for navigation around challenges that might send the organization in errant directions or even into total chaos? a mechanism that recognizes True North and whispers softly into your ear the correct direction to go when things get complicated.

The purpose of this work is to inform leaders (of schools, of all sectors) of a skillset that will allow them to naturally navigate their work environments as though they had a 'Leadership GPS.' This guiding information is the result of years of research regarding leadership and more recently, establishing a baseline theory on *LSI* via *leadership imprinting*.

Furthermore, the authors endorse the use of *the Leadership GPS model* to aid aspiring and current leaders better visualize their role in the organization. To assist in that role, *the LSI assessment* has been established. Its goal is to aid aspiring and current leaders in identifying their strengths and weaknesses in the principles of LSI. Additionally, with identification of strengths and weaknesses, willing leaders may be trained to enhance their natural LSI and if willing, be trained with *imprints* for new and effective skills to enhance the areas where improvement would be beneficial.

We further relate the model to keeping the organization moving in a *true north* fashion. This is done via analogies and character studies. We conclude with a discussion on the journey to becoming and remaining a successful leader.

The information in this book and the companion website are cutting-edge for the field of education. This work *specifically* includes the background and tools to transform leadership.

Introduction

Leadership Intelligence

Regardless of your political persuasion, the names of George W. Bush and Rudy Giuliani yield moving memories associated with the date of September 11, 2001. Their actions and reactions surrounding that point in time are indelibly imprinted on the minds of all Americans. And, although those two leaders faced a never before seen challenge, they responded with the leadership needed by the people of America during that time. They stood resolved, resilient, and believable. They stood as men of courage, tenacious and competent. They inspired us to believe in them and to believe in ourselves; they gave us hope for a better future.

Tom Menino, the mayor of Boston, after the horrific Marathon bombings displayed that same leadership ability. Knowing he was needed, he left his hospital bed to go to the aide of the victims and the city. As he shared later, "it's about leadership."[1] In the aforementioned events, those leaders, as well as countless others, were *imprinted* in that moment for dealing with extraordinary events in an extraordinary time.

Through the years, extraordinary events have inspired leaders to extraordinary action and galvanized our nation. As Tom Brokaw defined them, members of "The Greatest Generation"[2] faced an event of shattering proportions when the bombing of Pearl Harbor occurred. Leaders then, such as Franklin D. Roosevelt, held the rapt attention of the nation just as Bush and Giuliani did sixty years later.

During those sixty years, the nation and its leaders faced many trying times. Harry S. Truman led the nation out of World War II by making the unprecedented decision to employ nuclear weapons against Japan. John F. Kennedy moved the nation away from the brink of war by standing stalwart in the face of Soviet expansionism. Lyndon Johnson guided the nation to a new level of social responsibility in bringing forth the Civil Rights Act.

Ronald Reagan helped shatter the Berlin Wall and unite Germany through his ability to consummate a treaty with Mikhail Gorbachev.

The examples are numerous, but the key element in each instance is the same; leaders came to the forefront and displayed the Leadership Intelligence that carried the day. While few leaders will face the immense challenges of these leaders, all leaders face challenges large and small that call for the application of Leadership Intelligence.

It is in the day-to-day grind of carrying out his/her responsibilities that a leader gains the insights and skills allowing him/her to interact with people in a manner that establishes a bond of trust and respect. That bond allows a leader to build a bridge of trust putting all involved on the path that allows for success, like a GPS guiding you home, navigating to *your true north*. Finding the way to acquire those insights, master those skills, and build that bridge are the main thrusts of this book.

Part I

THE ROAD TRIP DEFINED

Chapter 1

Leadership Intelligence and Leadership Imprinting

Organizations today, as always, need strong, capable leaders. We need leaders with moxie and grit who are motivated to lead, who want to lead, and who are good at it. We need a cadre of influential leaders who are intrepid, not afraid to learn, and are willing to make decisions. We need people in 'the driver's seat' who are credible, competent, inspiring, visionary, and emotionally intelligent. We need leaders with Leadership Intelligence (LSI).

LSI is a construct that represents the level of leadership capacity an individual possesses at any given time. It addresses the characteristics, dispositions, and the 'soft' people/relational skills of individuals, including credibility, competence, ability to inspire, vision, and emotional intelligence. Within each of these five areas are specific subsets of characteristics, dispositions, or skills such as ethical behavior, discernibility, enthusiasm, commitment, and resilience (to name a few) that contribute to each component, respectively.

Often, these factors are unintentionally overlooked as a measure of leadership. Perhaps this is due to our lack of ability to assess them. And, while the cognitive ability (classical native intelligence) of the individual certainly plays a part in developing and applying LSI (assuming normal intelligence), it is not a controlling variable. Benjamin Bloom, an educational psychologist, related, "what any person in the world can learn, almost all persons can learn if provided with appropriate prior and current conditions of learning."[1]

Furthermore, many of the most valuable LSI constructs are rooted in the more primal areas of the human brain. Unlike the 'hard skills'—cognitive ability, analytical thinking, for example, which are learned via the 'new brain' or within the confines of the cerebrum—the most differentiating leadership skills of emotional intelligence, passion, and optimism (for example) are driven from the amygdala through the limbic region of the brain. This root variation suggests not only a completely different cerebral origin, but also a highly differentiated mechanism for learning and training in these functional areas.[2]

Possessing these qualities from birth (a genetic predisposition) or having them *imprinted*, or learning about them as an adolescent or young adult is a huge advantage for an aspiring leader. The ability of a leader to interact with his/her constituents in an effective manner is of utmost importance for job success.[3] And these abilities are not had by all, but are more and more being sought out by top-level CEOs for mid-level managers, as scores of studies are beginning to reveal that adeptness in these qualities are the things that push not only the individual, but the entire organization forward.[4]

The Graduate Management Council in 2014 reported that 71 percent of employers value emotional intelligence over IQ. It really doesn't make a difference whether the skillset is referred to as emotional intelligence as part of soft skills or actually competency in soft skills. Additionally, Business school alums shared that the top five skills utilized most on their jobs included interpersonal skills and conscientiousness. Furthermore, communication skills were ranked twice as important as managerial skills for newly hired employees.[5]

Other factors, of course, such as training and experience, contribute to the success of the leader as well. Certainly, current leadership preparation programs adequately prepare aspiring school leaders in the 'hard' skills such as budgetary/fiduciary management, curriculum design, instructional supervision, human resource management, and facilities management; however, these programs fall far short in addressing soft skills. Furthermore, experience enhances prior training or ongoing training (on-the-job or state required continuing education programs).

However, like classical native intelligence, training and experience are contributing but not controlling factors in leadership. The addition of LSI to a leader's repertoire can begin at any moment. In certain specific circumstances and conditions, a different type of learning that takes place is the basis of Leadership Intelligence. This different type of learning is called *imprinting*.

IMPRINTING

So, the age-old question—"Are leaders born or are leaders made?" Bloom provided one excellent answer in his remarks regarding all learning: 1 or 2 percent are "unusually capable," while 95 percent "can learn."[6] Howard Gardner's 1983 work on *Multiple Intelligences* aligns with Bloom and expands the answer to the question.[7] All people are born with gifts—intelligences. Some are gifted with spatial intelligence, others linguistic, and yet others with interpersonal intelligence. All are gifted with varying amounts of each of the intelligences. Some are born prodigies with the uncanny ability to play music with no lessons and without ever touching a single sheet of music. Others are mathematical geniuses. And some have gifts in more than one area but perhaps not so pointedly as a prodigy.

Some leaders are like that. They are gifted with a specific skillset that enables them to lead seemingly effortlessly, with confidence and charisma. These leaders are born with high levels of innate leadership potential and fall into the 1 or 2 percent who are unusually gifted. They learn easily and rapidly learn/develop and exhibit high levels of mastery in application of leadership skills and possess LSI. Others fall into the 95 percent who can and do learn, but at a more common pace, and they too possess and exhibit LSI. Followers of these leaders trust them, others gravitate to them. They are believable and likable; they are thoughtful and friendly. They are genuine. These leaders have learned how to be effective in an ongoing basis and display LSI. They have learned and developed LSI in the classical sense from instruction and experience. And there is yet a third group of leaders who have been thrust into a position of leadership but have not fully developed their leadership skills. These last two types of leaders (*made* slowly or swiftly) have gained LSI in a different way than *born* leaders. These leaders have been *imprinted* with LSI.

IMPRINTING: A HISTORICAL PERSPECTIVE

Imprinting as an act was first identified in the biological realm of the animals. The term was first coined by zoologist Konrad Lorenz in the early 1900s by observing ducklings and their tendency to follow the first thing they observed moving.[8] As these creatures first make their way into the world, they are 'imprinted' by their parents for survival. If by chance the mother duck is killed or otherwise unavailable for the duckling soon after birth, the duckling will attach itself to a surrogate parent for imprinting. The animal will then begin to mimic the behaviors it experiences with the surrogate parent.

A clear example of imprinting to a surrogate parent comes in the movie *Fly Away Home.*[9] In the screen adaption of the book *Father Goose* by Bill Lishman, goslings are orphaned when the mother goose is killed.[10] With no mother, the goslings imprint on a young girl named Amy. With her inventor father's help, Amy trains the goslings as they mature into young geese to follow an ultralight plane for their migration south, enabling the goslings to return to their natural lives.

An analogous yet different example of imprinting in the realm of the animal involves horses. In the last few decades, American horse enthusiasts have become very intrigued and taken by imprinting. The unborn colt may be influenced by humans in the womb of the mother. Furthermore, many of these same horse enthusiasts choose to be present at the birthing of the baby

horse, to continue the imprinting process. The process of touching, strok-
ing, and talking to the newborn foal creates gentler, more human-friendly
horses lacking the natural predatory fear of humans than their nonimprinted
counterparts.[11]

The key issues in Lorenz's and subsequent research on "imprinting or
imprinting like processes"[12] are that these processes occur during a sensitive
period, are relatively stable over time, and are a special type of learning.[13]

ORGANIZATIONAL AND HUMAN IMPRINTING

Moving beyond the biological realm and with the key features of imprinting
or imprinting-like processes in mind; the term 'imprinting' as used in organizational research and individual imprinting is based on the seminal work of
Arthur L. Stinchcombe. Even though he did not use the term, Stinchcombe is
generally credited with being the first to introduce the concept of imprinting
to organizational research.

In his essay *Social Structure and Organizations*,[14] Stinchcombe related
that new organizations tend to reflect the basal components present in the
environment in which they were formed and that once formed, those same
basal elements display great resistance to change over time. Put more simply,
the initial character and structure of an organization and the concomitant
processes, once formed, tend to remain the same or change only very slowly.
This same principle can be applied to individuals independently and as members of an organization.

Individuals can also be imprinted for all sorts of traits, among them leadership. Leadership knowledge (like all other content knowledge) is largely
gained through learning experiences, including intensive training, where the
would-be leader undergoes an experience as a practitioner in his/her chosen
field. And, as previously stated, although the plethora of theoretical knowledge informing the potential leader is useful and indeed informative, as are
interning leadership experiences, there is another form of learning experience, *imprinting*.

That is, the influence of seasoned leaders inspiring and advising future
leaders by planting seeds that will actually germinate through time and testing. Based on the above information and what we know about other leadership factors, we can derive that influences from childhood such as parents,
teachers, coaches, and ministers, as well as the lifelong growth and the matu-
ration process certainly have an influence on the emerging leader. Assuredly,
the training institution was a likely influence. Experience and mentoring
provide additional opportunities to incorporate new thinking and/or behaviors
into the overall performance repertoire.

While field experiences such as shadowing and internships undertaken during formal educational training are valuable tools for fostering experience and mentoring, it is not until a person fills the role as a leader that he or she experiences the full impact of the responsibilities that come with being a leader.[15] The quality (i.e., depth, scope, and breadth) of those early experiences is vital in developing the skills and abilities that allow those new to leadership to grow professionally and become successful both initially and in the long term (whether in the same or a different organization).

Much of what is gained in those training institution classroom settings may be put into practice based on cultivation of very early leadership experiences. Equally vital is having a leader who by example, word, and deed models appropriate leadership behavior and shares the processes and rationale for his or her decisions and actions with the neophyte leader. This oftentimes happens in the formal training stages of the aspiring leader.

As Kouzes so clearly points out:

> People become the leaders they observe. If we want to become good leaders, we have to see good leaders.
>
> To increase the quality and supply of exemplary leaders in the world, it's essential to give aspiring talent the chance to observe models of exemplary leadership. To develop ethical leaders, allow aspiring talent to observe leaders behaving ethically. To build leaders who think long-term, allow aspiring talent to observe leaders taking a long-term view. To have leaders who treat people with dignity and respect, make sure aspiring talent can observe leaders' treating people with dignity and respect.
>
> It's absolutely essential to the growth and development of leaders—or of anyone, for that matter—that they're exposed to the behaviors they're expected to produce. You can't do what you say if you don't know how, and you can't know how until you can *see* how it's done. Without exemplary role models, all the training in the world won't stick.[16]

Almost all leaders start at the entry level. The few exceptions are rare and generally involve succession of heirs to proprietary enterprises. For all of those whose career brings them to a leadership position there are periods of time when they are beginning the process of becoming a leader. These early career stages are 'periods' rather than transitions. Perhaps, these moments in time are when the aspiring leader is 'ready' to be taught.

Marquis and Tilcsik in their investigation and examination on human imprinting further emphasize this point.[17] In their studies, they posit there are many times when learning takes place, but not all of it 'sticks.' By such mechanisms, beginning leaders become acclimated to the organizational expectations and the individual skills necessary for success in that organization.[18] This acclimation or process has been described in other disciplines as imprinting or career imprinting. In 2005, in her book *Career Imprints: Creating Leaders across an Industry*, Higgins shares that "senior managers and leaders are shaped by people—a mentor, role model, even an adversary—and by organizations in which they work."[19]

HOW LEADERSHIP IMPRINTING OCCURS

As stated earlier, imprinting can happen in three ways. In their work, Marquis and Tilcsik advanced a three-part definition of imprinting that emphasizes:

- Brief sensitive periods of transition during which the focal entity exhibits high susceptibility to external influences (such as those with Lorenz' ducks);
- A process whereby the focal entity comes to reflect elements of its environment during a sensitive period, what educators call 'in the teachable moment'; and
- The persistence of imprints despite subsequent environmental changes.[20]

For born leaders, this could be a genetic predisposition toward leadership. We have all witnessed young children playing when one exerts the 'leader' role and the others follow. A later example of the brief sensitive period might be the first leadership position an individual holds in an organization when he/she exhibits high susceptibility to external influences or when the leader moves to different position within or external to the organization. It might be even earlier, perhaps when the individual is elected as president of the junior class in high school.

Perhaps a reflection of environmental elements might include the neophyte leader adopting the practices of leaders he/she has observed or been exposed to when a specific moment arrives. Having no experience of their own to reflect on, they recall how someone they admire reacted to a similar situation.

And finally, the leader may acknowledge his/her own limitations and choose to receive training (which, in the case of *imprinting*, takes a good deal of commitment and time). A true leader will recognize strengths and weaknesses in their role and will choose to grow to become better in their role.

Furthermore, to 'undo' an imprint would be an equally difficult task; think of removing a tattoo. Imprints are very persistent but with work may be unlearned. As Semsik et al. point out:

> The kernel of the imprinting hypothesis, first advanced by Stinchcombe (1965), is that characteristics of an entity shaped during a sensitive moment of its existence can persist for decades, in spite of subsequent environmental changes

(Johnson, 2007; Marquis, 2003). Evidence shows that imprinted organizational structures (Johnson, 2007), strategies (Boeker, 1989a), philosophies (Harris & Ogbonna, 1999), and policies (Burton & Beckman, 2007) hold explanatory power even when accounting for contemporaneous influences.[21]

Additionally, Semsik relates in his review of imprinting, however, that

mechanisms that lead to imprint decay include distant organizational search (Kriauciunas & Kale), incremental contextual and component changes (Datta et al., 2003; Jones, 2001), aging and poor performance (Boeker, 1989a), changes in the management team (Beckman, Burton, & O'Reilly, 2007), memory erosion (Dimov et al., 2012; Gulati, 1995), mismatches between the imprint and larger institutional realities (Kimberly, 1979), and competitive pressures to converge to best practices (Cockburn, Henderson, & Stern, 2000).[22]

Semsik also provides a hypothetical mechanism whereby imprinting occurs. He states that "research suggests a distinction between the process by which imprints are formed and the subsequent mechanisms by which they evolve."[23] Operationally, the framework Simsek proposes is straightforward. Imprinting occurs when an *imprinter* is in association with or in close proximity to the person undergoing imprinting. Circumstances allow imprinting to occur. The imprint dynamics relate to the "path duration and evolution of imprints," while the impact of imprints is dependent upon the interaction of the individual, the setting within the organization, and elements external to the organization.[24]

Whatever the specific mechanism, imprinting is a special type of learning that occurs in social organizational settings, and the learning that occurs is both substantial and persistent in its impact. According to Tilcsik:

At the individual level, imprinting research suggests that the conditions experienced in the early years of organizational tenure or a career exert a lasting influence on subsequent habits, routines, and behaviors. Imprinting has been documented in a variety of settings.[25]

For example, consider the apprentice school administrator in training. A middle school student reports to his parent (who also happens to be a school employee) that one of the teachers is 'surfing the internet' looking for dates during her planning period. As her student aide for that period, he is frequently asked his opinion regarding potential 'on-line matches.' The stunned and unhappy parent of the student approaches the principal with the information.

The principal, in an attempt to help educate the 'apprentice administrator' brings him/her in on the conversation with the licentious teacher. Having received a quick briefing, the 'would-be administrator' is anxious about the upcoming meeting between the principal and the teacher. This apprentice is prepared for the fireworks.

The teacher is sent a note from the school principal for a 'visit to the office' during her planning period. The note has no explanation for the meeting. On her planning period, the teacher arrives. The principal is calm and inviting as the teacher enters the office. 'You needed to see me?' the teacher asks. Rather than an explosive outburst, the principal calmly says to the teacher, 'yes, Ms. So-and-so, I do. We have a problem and I need your help solving it.'

Talk about leaving an imprint. The administrative intern went into the conference expecting 'Clash of the Titans' and left hearing the teacher take ownership of the problem and even suggesting solutions to correct the issue. This is an example of learning a lesson in the moment so profoundly that it leaves the novice with an *imprint, a* great *imprint.* This type of imprint is referred to as a 'stress imprint' as it has come in an unexpected manner. Furthermore, this type of imprint is one that the novice will call on over and over in his/her own administrative career.

STRESS IMPRINTS, DESIRED IMPRINTS, AND MENTORING

Imprinting is not mentoring, although they do have some of the same elements. Generally speaking, mentoring is intentional and planned. It is rarely a one-time event. Stress imprinting is specific incident that happens at a specific point in time and can be recalled specifically. It generally is a very profound incident. This type of imprinting is very different than mentoring.

Desired imprints, however, are similar to mentoring in that they are intentional and planned. Creating an imprint is a very basal type of training (from the core area of the brain) and thus must be repeated over and over for learning to occur. As Tilcsik stated, "Although the characteristics of early peers and mentors are undoubtedly important, they represent only one dimension of the richly textured intra-organizational environment in which socialization takes place—in addition to factors like the economic environment, the intra-organizational competitive landscape, or the network structural position in which a newcomer operates."[26]

Whether learning in a more conventional manner or imprinted, LSI allows a leader to move through the tasks, interactions with other individuals and entities with ease and a sense of confidence. It often seems as if the successful leader has an unfailing GPS to guide him/her as he/she navigates to success as a leader.

Chapter 2

The Leadership GPS Model

The Leadership GPS model serves as a three-dimensional representation of moving an object from a beginning point to a desired location. In the case of an organization, the leader guides the organization toward its goals much as the driver maneuvers the automobile to the destination in travel. In the same way, that a GPS enhances the ability of the driver to arrive at a never before traveled destination, the Leadership Intelligence (LSI) skillset assists a leader in guiding an organization toward its goals.

When you consider a person making a trip in an automobile equipped with a GPS, your mind actually visualizes a car, a driver, and a GPS. As such, in thinking of a leader guiding an organization to its *true north* destiny, we would like for you to visualize a compass superimposed by a gyroscope standing atop a base of LSI constructs. These analogies are expounded upon over the next few pages.

The model helps us to conceptualize the leader moving an organization toward a particular set of goals and getting feedback or direction along the way via the GPS. In this model, the organization is represented by the *compass*, the leader by the *gyroscope*, and LSI by a base on which both stand.

HOW DOES THE LEADERSHIP GPS MODEL WORK?

Organizations

Most organizations are guided by a vision and mission statement. These are generally broken into organizational *goals* that give the organization its direction. The organization (for the Leadership GPS model) is represented by a *compass*. Although any compass can give a reading on direction, it cannot orient itself to a particular direction of its own accord.

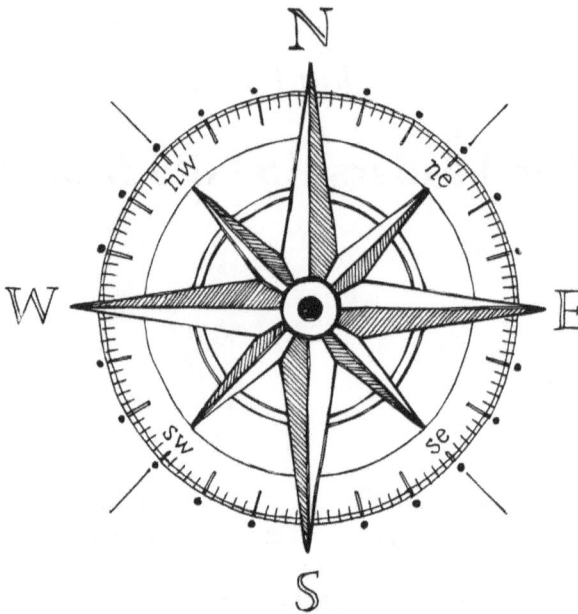

Figure 2.1   The Organization is Represented by a Compass.

A compass without someone to read it and follow the course it sets is like an automobile without a driver. Although the automobile has the capacity to go anywhere, it will go nowhere without a driver. Likewise, an organization with the most lofty and noble goals will travel nowhere without a savvy leader. In more generic terms, automobiles were created to take people to places. However, without an astute driver, the vehicle may end up at the end of a dead-end street. The symbolic direction for the auto (and the organization) to take is north, *true north*.

In the book *True North* by George and Sims, 125 leaders were interviewed to find their common characteristics.[1] One of the revelations was how critically those leaders' lives were influenced by significant others (who were also leaders) and how important the significant other's personal stories were in shaping those leaders. This is another example of leadership *imprinting*.

Time after time those interviewed describe a turning point in their lives that transformed them into the leaders they were (are) today. These tales reveal their most deeply held values, their most passionate beliefs. Such autobiographical stories continue to inspire the leaders who lived them, keeping their moral compasses pointed toward *true north*.

In the foreword of the same book, Gergen made this remark: "What ultimately distinguishes the great leaders from the mediocre are the personal inner qualities—qualities that are hard to define but are essential for success, qualities that each of us must develop for ourselves."[2] (In this context, the authors are referring to *true north* qualities.)

In reference to former President Ronald Reagan, Gergen says, "Reagan, like Ford, had figured out who he was and liked it. He didn't just feel comfortable in his own skin; he felt serene. Reagan not only had a compass for his life but a compass for his political beliefs, and he communicated both with a contagious optimism that stirred people across the land."

Of former President Bill Clinton, Gergen said, "my sense is that Clinton's central problem has been the lack of an inner compass. He has 360-degree vision but no true north. He isn't yet fully grounded within."[3]

Continuing in the foreword to *True North*, Gergen states that "ability matters to a president, but inner qualities matter even more. As historian David McCullough wrote in assessing the leadership of Harry Truman: 'Character is the single most important asset of a president.' I would add this thought: that character without capacity usually means weakness in a leader, but capacity without character means danger."[4]

In the sequel to *True North* (*True North: Discover Your Authentic Leadership*), George and Peter Sims make the persuasive argument that the journey toward authentic leadership—finding your own *true north*—is the key to leadership in all fields. Indeed, this is the case.

In organizations (as well as in our individual lives) we want to dwell at *true north* but we are rarely ever exactly there. If our organizations (or we ourselves) are *close* to true north, we are in a pretty good place. Think of times when your finances weren't strained, your health was good, your stress was at an acceptable level, and you were at the top of your game. Ah, life *near* true north.

And, truly, if your organization (or your life) has been in chaos, or even somewhat chaotic, getting near north (some sort of normalcy) feels really good. Think of a time when a close friend or family member may have been hospitalized for a short while. Every day you did your best to stop by and visit the person to encourage them and lift their spirits. Now, reflect on what it was like *not* to have to stop by the hospital every day after work. Although you wanted to be an encourager, it felt *good* not to need to make a stop anymore.

When the organization (or again, our personal life) is at *true north* or near north (let's say NNE or NNW), then it can be considered to be in a good static state (homeostasis). However, over time, we can become complacent or apathetic in a static state. So, back to the earlier hospital scenario. Two weeks after the daily hospital visits are over, we have forgotten how stressful the experience was, we become comfortable once again with our routine. We find that even though we could do more (we did it when we went by the hospital everyday), now, we accept just a little less; just to be close to true north is 'enough.'

However, as Collins shared in his book, *Good to Great*, "good is the opposite of great."[5] The ultimate goal for any leader (or any individual) is to be at our best—but 'best' is difficult to maintain. That is often why we set goals, to stretch ourselves, to keep from becoming complacent. So the organization (or person in the examples above) should *always strive* to be at *true north (*even when they are *near* north*)*. Again, this is not to say the organization/person is always there, but, again, should always *be striving* to be there.

As a recap, as an automobile can transport passengers, organizations move individuals. Think again about the automobile GPS analogy. The symbolic destination for both the automobile and the organization is *true north*. With the mechanism for transporting or moving entities, we now need a component to move each toward the destination. In the case of the automobile, we have a driver, and for the organization, a leader.

LEADERS

Earlier we stated that every organization, metaphorically, wants to be headed north. As you will recall, the organization in the Leadership GPS model is represented by a compass. Although a compass is a very good gauge of north, there are better indicators. As a matter of fact, a gyroscope in motion is an extremely precise instrument for north—*true north.* The gyroscope is such an accurate device that it is utilized in the Hubble telescope as well as in intercontinental ballistic missiles. A gyroscope set in motion is an extremely precise instrument.

An organization needs a leader to move it forward. As the driver is for the car, the leader is for the organization. The role of the leader is to keep the organization focused near north (toward its organizational goals). The organization needs a savvy leader to handle that responsibility. Think, for example, of the daily routine at an elementary school building. The cafeteria can run short on food, a water fountain can spring a huge leak, three teachers can call in sick, only two substitutes can be found, and Bus #36 can have a flat tire, all in the same morning.

Keeping the compass (organization) focused between NNE to NNW (or 22.5 degrees +/- N) would be pretty impressive in that scenario on a daily basis. But, it routinely happens and oftentimes even more. School leaders have been *trained* to deal with these types of scenarios. Leaders have something internal that guides them to handle the day-to-day crises. And that something is more than a guiding compass. Leaders have been etched (or imprinted, if you will) with a 'core' gyroscope. They have at their disposal a mechanism that helps them identify and 'hone in on' *true north.*

In fact, in the Leadership GPS model, the leader acts as the *gyroscope.*

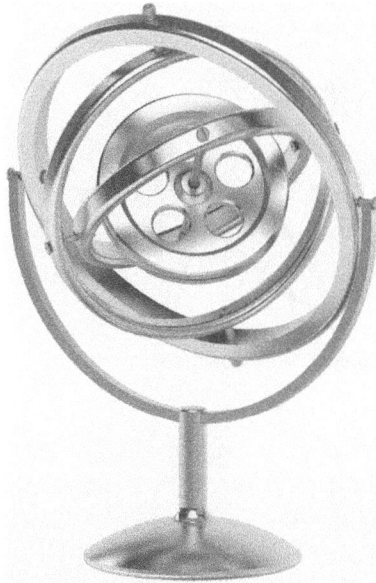

Figure 2.2 The Leader is Represented by a Gyroscope.

The organization (or compass) alone has no *centeredness*; it is only an amalgamation of all of the parts within it, or as a compass, it only has a magnetic field that can demonstrate deviation from north. The leader, however, is a living being. As a gyroscope is a much greater predictor of direction than a compass, a leader can more easily detect movement away from organizational priorities than can the organization itself.

IN TANDEM

Below is the Leadership GPS model of the gyroscope (*leader*) superimposed over the compass (*organization*) ensuring that it stays the course.

In figure 2.3, rather than acting as two independent mechanisms, the leader and the organization are conjoined and interdependent. The leader (gyroscope) sits over the organization (compass) working diligently to ensure it maintains its *true north*ward orientation. Reflecting to the earlier example, where the school principal (leader) dealt with several actions at one time (with perhaps none of them having to do with the central mission and vision of the organization), the leader was able to skillfully resolve the issues and keep things running smoothly.

We might similarly describe this as the organization tipping toward the NNE or NNW quadrants of the compass while the gyroscope holds them

Figure 2.3   The Leader Guides the Organization.

tightly on course. And as stated earlier, NNE to NNW (22.5 degrees +/–
north) is an absolutely great place to be. However, what happens when
the compass (organization) moves more violently in one direction or the
other due to encountering more extreme circumstances? What if the organization swiftly shifts in an easterly direction or yet worse, due south—the
antithesis—of *true north*?

When the system moves toward *east* or *west* (actually anything beyond
22.5 degrees +/– N), it is moving in a problematic direction and therefore, a
systematic correction of a time sensitive nature is necessary (by the leader).
If we were actually traveling in an automobile (GPS on), headed in a north-
erly direction and then unexpectedly took off in an errant direction, the GPS
would begin to sound off.

Initially, in a car, the GPS might not recognize a slight deviation. However, as the driver moves further off course, the GPS would ask for a turn at
the next opportunity to get back on course. If the driver continues down the
wrong path, the GPS would either redirect the driver or completely create a
new course (the infamous 'recalculating') due to the errant path.

If (worst-case scenario) an organization heads *south* or in a *southerly*
direction, the organization would be considered to be in a state of complete
chaos. *All hands on deck. The system is in disarray. Armageddon.* In our organizational analogy, the leader would be responsible to *turn the organization
around.* But, what if the leader has *no idea* how to do this and has *never traveled* in this direction before? He/she, however, may or may not (at this point)
have the skillset to move the organization back on course. In this situation,
the leader appears to need assistance.

As in a vehicle, if we are traveling in unfamiliar territory, we may feel the
need to turn on the GPS for route assistance. If we are heading into territory
we have never traveled before, we will make better decisions with more information. For example, you are expecting an interaction with the media this

afternoon due to a new marketing campaign, and are putting the final touches in place for that event. You have no idea that a boiler in your building will explode at 3:00 p.m. and will claim the lives of four innocent people. This is completely unchartered territory.

THE LSI SKILLSET

It is at times like these (being in unfamiliar territory) when a GPS might come in handy. In the day-to-day activities of your job, the idea is to keep the organization in the 22.5 degrees +/− N zone. But when confronted with a completely new situation (or a new destination, by the GPS analogy), you can choose to rely on your instincts, take directions from others, or plug in the LSI skillset. For the leader, *Leadership Intelligence* is the ticket. It is readily accessible for the *born* leader. However, *for the leader who is 'made,'* the LSI skillset is as critical a tool as the GPS is to the driver who is lost.

LSI gives directions based on imprints just as a GPS gives directions based on satellites. As mentioned earlier, some leaders are born with these imprints, while some leaders must learn them. The directions that are given are based on the imprint that is needed for the current route. As a GPS won't tell you to dodge the large piece of tire rubber in the road, these imprints will not equip the leader with common sense or the ability to make judgments. What the skillset does, is give needed direction to the leader regarding the decision options available.

Much like a GPS in an automobile, LSI is the information (or skillset) the leader needs in order to reach the final destination of *true north*. This happens by birth or by choice. A GPS does not give the driver information unless the driver elects to turn it on. Again, for some leaders, the information is second nature because they were naturally *imprinted*. For the other 95 percent, learning the directions (skillset) is a work-in-progress.

LSI is analogous to an actual GPS as an intellectual tool. After a person has traveled the route a few times, they no longer need the assistance of the GPS. But, always, when traveling in new territory, guidance is needed and that is what the GPS (LSI) does—offers suggestions and guidance. However, ultimately, it is the leader who still must make the decisions.

The astute leader will choose to use the LSI (as a driver uses a GPS):

- When the leader is traveling in unfamiliar territory;
- When the leader has not been to a place in a long time and perhaps it is very different now;
- When the leader wants to identify all of the potential different routes;

- To get an idea of how long it will take to make it to the new destination;
- To navigate around in a new place

One nontangible ancillary characteristic of leadership *imprints* is what we have come to call *soft skills* in the work world. They are skills or abilities that 'born leaders' possess having observed or 'learned' from the *imprints* of those before them. Those same *imprints* can be taught and are a highly critical skillset for success in positions of leadership.

Table 2.1 lists the *LSI skillset* that will be described in detail in the following chapters. These competencies are the *imprints* needed for successful leadership. These are skills or abilities you can enjoy as your own. You may already have a modicum of some, many, or all, of these skills. You can also improve in some, many, or all, of these skills.

The words or phrases beneath each of the headings in table 2.1 that follow are descriptors for measuring effective LSI in each of the skill/disposition areas. The LSI assessment (based on this table) can be utilized to evaluate the level of skill (via self-report) in each area. More effectively, it can be utilized as a tool for 360 feedback, eliciting responses from peers, subordinates, and supervisors for a more realistic assessment of the LSI skillset had by an individual.

Completing the assessment allows one to see areas of strength as well as areas of relative weakness. Maintaining or enhancing areas of strength while improving areas of relative weakness requires further action. And, while there are many options, ultimately, the best option for an emerging leader is to learn how to enhance skills across the board but with emphasis in the areas where the most work is needed.*

LSI SKILLSET

Skill enhancement begins with a clear understanding of the skillset leaders need to succeed. With that understanding as a base to build upon, an aspiring leader can seek out opportunities to enhance his/her skillset. But it all starts with knowing where you are currently and making the decision to move forward to enhanced LSI and success. The following chapters will help build that understanding with GPS analogies and real-life examples. Then the decision is up to you.

---

* For more information on improving these skillsets, go to www.leadershipintelligencelsi.com

Table 2.1 The Five Leader Imperatives of the Leadership GPS Model

Credibility *In five hundred feet, stay right*	**Competence** *Recalculating*	**Inspiration** *Lost satellite reception*	**Vision** *Arriving at your destination*	**Emotional Intelligence** *Route guidance suggested*
Ethics or personal accountability	Discernibility	Enthusiastic	Commitment	Resilience
Honesty	Perception	Energetic	Sense of direction	Communication and listening
Responsibility	Conflict resolution skills	Passionate	Professionalism	Happiness
Trust	Problem-solving and decision-making skills	Optimistic	Decisive	Personality traits
Integrity	Relationship building	Genuine	Work ethic	Sense of humor
Sincerity	Planning and implementation	Courageous	Concern for the future	Assertiveness
	Assessment and evaluation			Flexibility
				Empathy/inter-personal interactions

Part II

GPS ROUTE GUIDANCE AVAILABLE

Chapter 3

'In Five Hundred Feet, Stay Right'

Leader Credibility

'In five hundred feet, stay right?' This seems more of a common-sense directive than a GPS analogy, and it is. Why? Because we expect our leaders to always *stay right*. We expect them to make the *right* choices, do the *right* thing, behave in the *right* way, go to the *right* places, and know the *right* people. We look for our leaders to *be right*. And *rightness* gives them credibility. Does this mean that leaders who do not wear the right clothes or always have the *right* words are not credible or less credible? Certainly not.

However, a study by *Salary for Business.com* shares many valuable points regarding dress, including the remark that "people who dress professionally act more professional on the job. Dressing in jeans and a t-shirt does not exude professionalism, especially when you are seated in close proximity to an executive in a business suit."[1] In this same study, the majority of respondents admitted they make assumptions about people based on the way they are dressed.

With regard to saying the right thing, in *The Top Complaints from Employees About Their Leaders*, "91 percent of employees say communication issues can drag executives down."[2] So, credibility is not only about *being* credible, it is also about others *believing* that you *have* credibility.

Moreover, it's not just about the clothes a leader wears or what he/she says. Consider the leader who has a commitment to his/her religious beliefs such that he/she acts accordingly—for example, they refuse to schedule activities on Wednesday nights due to potential church activity conflicts. This attitude as opposed to the leader who does not share this belief system may schedule an occasional Sunday workday (or the like). Some would regard these belief systems as a show of credibility.

We want our leaders to have a belief system that we can admire—one that we believe is credible. If we have a leader who is a member of a discriminatory or elitist group, or who holds wildly radical political views, or perhaps is a member of an organized 'swingers' club, we tend to have questions regarding their credibility.

So how do you attain *credibility* if you haven't enjoyed it before? Some of the ways to create the perception that you are credible have been alluded to above. Dress, speech, attitude, affiliations; all of these are a part of helping others have a willingness to put their trust in you as a leader. But credibility is much deeper than these things.

Credibility is a word that always seems to conjure up images of a constant striving. In the competitive, 'what-have-you-done-for-me-lately' work environment when leaders must be like magicians and always be ready to pull the next 'rabbit out of the hat' (the next big creation, innovation, and project), leaders are often only as good as their last successful undertaking. Developing and maintaining credibility is a career-long and more often than not, life-long pursuit. Kouzes and Posner, highly regarded authors on leadership, state:

> What we found quite unexpectedly in our initial research and have reaffirmed ever since is that, above all else, people want leaders who are credible. We want to believe in our leaders. We want to have faith and confidence in them as people. We want to believe that their word can be trusted, that they have the knowledge and skill to lead, and that they are personally excited and enthusiastic about the direction in which we are headed. Credibility is the foundation of leadership.[3]

Comments like those of Kouzes and Posner extolling the importance of leader credibility can be found throughout the literature. Brian Leavy, former Dean of the Dublin City University School of Business, shared that "all great leaders recognise credibility as the dynamic currency of leadership."[4] DePuy holds that "successful leadership relies heavily on three factors, trust, credibility, and respect, which he refers to as the 'linchpins of success.'"[5]

Stephen Covey in discussing what he described as the four roles of leadership stated, "The first role is simply to be an example, a model: one whose life has credibility with others, has integrity, diligence, humility, the spirit of servant-leadership, of contribution. This is the most fundamental of our roles."[6] Ken Blanchard in his book, *The Secret*, related, "For a leader to be successful, he or she must embody the values of their organization. So, if you are leading at your child's school or in your church, you should embody the values of that particular organization. The power is in the trust and credibility you build."[7]

Walter Cronkite was the news anchorman for the CBS Evening News in the 1960s and 1970s. He was often cited as 'the most trusted man in America.' His composure during the Kennedy assassination was one of many events that merited Cronkite that title. In the late 1960s, Cronkite made a trip to Vietnam in order to report to America what was truly happening on the ground.

During his broadcast, he said, "To say that we are closer to victory today is to believe, in the face of the evidence, the optimists who have been wrong in the past. But it is increasingly clear to this reporter that the only rational way out then will be to negotiate, not as victors, but as an honorable people who lived up to their pledge to defend democracy, and did the best they could." His reporting was so credible that then president Lyndon B. Johnson shared, "If I've lost Cronkite, I've lost the country."[8]

As significant as credibility is to leadership it is equally fragile. Credibility is as easily lost as it is hard to gain. Kaipa said, "When your words and actions don't align, you have fallen into the Credibility Gap. When you have a credibility gap at your workplace, it is damaging to your reputation and to your career. And if you're in a leadership or customer service role, your credibility gap could be hurting your company."[9]

DePuy related that "trust, credibility, and respect can be destroyed in a day, often taking years to rebuild—meanwhile, employee engagement is evaporating and the mission suffering."[10] Leaders remain credible as long as experiences and the passage of time confirm that their assertions, and related decisions, are/were in line with the requirements of circumstances. While major blunders/missteps can obviously negatively impact credibility even small missteps can have less than positive consequences. As Kouzes makes explicit in an example from an interview session:

> One of the things I write and talk about a lot is personal credibility. Credibility is the foundation of all leadership. I was talking about it in front of a group of about 3,000 store managers from around the country at a big retail organization's annual conference. I was making a point about being competent, and I was referring to the CEO of this company by his first name: Let's call him Dan. I would say, "As Dan said," because I had the opportunity to interview him before the event. Then, about the third time I quoted him, someone in the back said, "It's David." I had been misspeaking the whole time, and it was very embarrassing! But it was a wonderful learning opportunity to point out to the audience that I had been talking about credibility, and I had just diminished my own by calling somebody by the wrong name. Sometimes the best lessons in life come when you screw up.[11]

Similarly, in a 2014 race at the Talladega Superspeedway, Dale Earnhardt Jr. lost his track position when he chose to pit. Back on the track, the NASCAR superstar found himself in thirteenth position. Rather than making a move to get back into the thick of the race, he laid back most of the entire last thirty laps of the race. To Earnhardt, it seemed the wise thing to do.

Having suffered a concussion in 2012, it didn't appear to be plausible to mix it up in the tight Talladega which is known for its big wrecks. But, there were no big pile-ups on this day and his loyal fan base was not happy. One of his supporters remarked, "So why should I and thousands of other fans pay to see someone who does not feel like racing? Remind me, please."[12] Again, credibility is fragile, and as much as Junior's fans love him, on this day they were not happy with him.

The LSI model addresses credibility as being based on a leader having a well-grounded sense of ethics, honesty, responsibility, trustworthiness, integrity, and being sincere in interactions with others. These characteristics are what tend to set highly successful leaders, those with high LSI, apart. Importantly, the habits and dispositions on which credibility is based can be taught or observed, learned, and imprinted. The following characteristics embody the knowledge and skills need for building credibility.

ETHICS OR PERSONAL ACCOUNTABILITY

If 'no news is good news,' then it is best not to access any media source, including obtaining news the old-fashioned way by reading a newspaper. One look at most any media source will almost surely detail yet another embarrassing failure of a leader. Leadership failures (as with nonleaders) run the gamut of offenses from unlawful acts to ploys that are questionable morally and ethically (deeds that shock the conscience but are not illegal), to the sheer inability to get the job done.

Leaders who commit unlawful acts lose whatever credibility they had completely and, in all likelihood, will never regain it. There are rare exceptions such as Martha Stewart who returned to a prominent role in her company Martha Stewart Living Omni media and also with the National Broadcasting Company after her conviction for insider trading and subsequent imprisonment.[13]

Leaders who commit questionable acts (that are not unlawful) lose credibility but at times will receive a second chance. This was the case for General George Patton being reinstated and leading the US Third Army during World War II.[14] On the other hand, many who commit questionable acts do not receive a second chance. Such was the case for Donald Sterling, who lost control of the National Basketball Association's Los Angeles Clippers over racist remarks he made.[15] The Clippers moved on without Sterling.

Mark Hurd, formerly of Hewlett-Packard, "learned the hard way that when you're the man in charge, even somewhat minor misdeeds can get you the boot." Hurd stepped down from his post as chief executive officer of Hewlett-Packard on August 6, 2010, after the company found "he submitted inaccurate expense reports that concealed his personal relationship with a female contractor who assisted on HP-sponsored events."[16] Hewlett-Packard moved on but without Hurd.

The leaders in the last category are those who are unable to get the job done (or those perceived as not having lived up to expectations but still may be salvageable as leaders). These are the ones who are said to have become derailed and have also lost credibility. Often, however, they have a chance of regaining their credibility, especially if they change positions or organizations.

In either case, these leaders have forgotten the most basic principle in life, *do what is right*. Drucker in discussing effective leaders asked the question, "So what do effective leaders have in common?" And answered the question by saying, "They get the right things done, in the right ways."[17]

Billy Graham, often dubbed as 'America's preacher,' began revival crusades in the deep south in the 1947.[18] He was so respected for his ethics and personal accountability that he served as religious council to decades of US presidents. Among the things that won Graham his place in American and even world history was his undying kindness and respect.

Although initially he was met with great resistance from jeering crowds to hate mail and even being pelted with projectiles, he always responded in kindness. Graham determined early in his crusade ministry that his crusades would never be segregated. This was very unpopular at the time but indicated his deep sense of moral and ethical values.

Doing what is right begins with ethical behavior and personal accountability. Ethical behavior has the connotation of behavior that is morally acceptable. What is morally acceptable—not in the sense of denominational religious/spiritual beliefs (though that might be true as well)—but in terms of the normative morally acceptable behaviors, mores, of a given society, or organization?

In that regard, Langvardt holds that leaders play "dual roles . . . regarding matters of ethics: they are students in the sense that they learn, or should learn, from relevant experiences (both their own and those of others); and, through the examples they set, they are teachers of other persons affiliated with the organization and of non-affiliated persons who observe their actions."[19] With ethical behavior, as with most other leader behavior, it is important to understand and accept that leaders are public figures.

The old truism, "we learn what to do as well as what not to do," is certainly applicable. Leaders learn or can be imprinted with ethical behavior (as well as unethical, but that is a study for another day). That being said, leaders can also develop the ability to accurately judge whether a specific statement or action is ethical and to sense when others may question the ethical nature of a statement or action. They can develop and internalize a sense of doing what is right. That sense can then be used to navigate, with great dexterity, through any problem/issue.

Personal accountability is the simultaneous process in judging whether leader behavior is ethical. No leader is perfect. Missteps will occur. Hopefully those missteps will be few and infrequent. But when they happen, the ethical leader is accountable for his/her actions. They do not blame others or circumstances. The words, "that was my decision and I am accountable for it," make a difference to those within and external to an organization.

Galindo describes personal accountability in this way, "Unlike responsibility (the *before*) and self-empowerment (the *during*), personal accountability is the *after*. It's a willingness—after all is said and done—to answer for the outcomes of your choices, actions, and behaviors. When you're personally accountable, you stop assigning blame, 'shouldering' on people, and making excuses. Instead, you take the fall when your choices cause problems."[20]

As a leader, ethically and in terms of personal accountability, it is best to choose to *do what is right* as best as what is *right* can be determined. Then bask in the glow of a prudent decision leading to success. Or, if the decision fails to deliver the desired results, or worse exacerbates a problem, accept the criticism that comes. Criticism, like credibility is a source of learning.

HONESTY

Doing what is right also means being honest. Being honest in itself is a requisite characteristic of a leader who is credible. It is also a requisite characteristic for colleagues, or for that matter for all members of an organization. The importance of honesty is emphasized by Kouzes and Posner, who report that "in an ongoing project surveying tens of thousands of working people around the world, we asked, 'What do you look for and admire in a leader (defined as someone whose direction you would willingly follow)?' Then we asked, 'What do you look for and admire in a colleague (defined as someone you'd like to have on your team)?' The number one requirement of a leader—honesty—was also the top-ranking attribute of a good colleague."[21]

O'Toole and Bennis see honesty as related to transparency and share that "No organization can be honest with the public if it's not honest with itself. But being honest inside an organization is more difficult than it sounds. People hoard information, engage in groupthink, tell their boss only what they think he/she wants to hear, and ignore facts that are staring them in the face."[22] To counter these natural tendencies, leaders need to make a conscious decision to support transparency and create a culture of candor. Organizations that fail to achieve transparency will have it forced upon them. There's just no way to keep a lot of secrets in the age of the internet.[23]

They go on to outline recommended steps to establish a 'culture of candor':

If you want to develop a culture of candor, start with your own behavior and then work outward—and keep these recommendations in mind.

Tell the truth. We all have an impulse to tell people what they want to hear. Wise executives tell everyone the same unvarnished story. Once you develop a reputation for straight talk, people will return the favor.

Encourage people to speak truth to power. It's extraordinarily difficult for people lower in a hierarchy to tell higher-ups unpalatable truths—but that's what the higher-ups need to know, because often their employees have access to information about problems that they don't. Create the conditions for people to be courageous.

Reward contrarians. Your company won't innovate successfully if you don't learn to recognize, then challenge your own assumptions. Find colleagues who can help you do that. Promote the best of them. Thank all of them.

Practice having unpleasant conversations. The best leaders learn how to deliver bad news kindly so that people don't get unnecessarily hurt. That's not easy—so find a safe place to practice.

Diversify your sources of information. Everyone's biased. Make sure you communicate regularly with different groups of employees, customers, and competitors, so that your own understanding is nuanced and multifaceted.

Admit your mistakes. This gives everyone around you permission to do the same.

Build organizational support for transparency. Start with protection for whistle-blowers, but don't stop there. Hire people because they created a culture of candor elsewhere (not because they can outcompete their peers).

Set information free. Most organizations default to keeping information confidential when it *might* be strategic or private. Default, instead, to sharing information—unless there's a clear reason not to.[24]

When a leader establishes his/her honesty by being accountable and doing what is right, he/she will be able to create the 'culture of candor' suggested. It is in making honesty and truth a *sine qua non* of an organization that true progress toward success is made. At the same time, it is always well to be reminded that civility is still necessary in speaking candidly. Civility requires the thoughtful consideration of what is to be said or done and is built on honesty as an element of credibility.

RESPONSIBILITY

Responsibility is that element in social/organizational interaction that identifies that for which a leader will be held personally accountable. As Galindo shared, "When you're truly responsible, you believe that success or failure is up to you, even if you work within a team or are blindsided by unforeseen circumstances. You own your commitment to a result before the fact—before you even take action."[25]

The commitment on which responsibility is based produces ownership and imbues meaning to a task. For leaders, responsibility has many facets, including what is done individually and what is established through the mission and goals of the organization that others carry out. As the sign on President Harry Truman's desk famously said, "The Buck Stops Here."[26] Responsibility like ethical behavior and personal accountability *can be* learned or imprinted.

One such example can be found in Pat Summitt, former head women's basketball coach at the University of Tennessee. Summitt was one of the most respected coaches in the history of the sport, not only for her winning record, but also due to her sense of responsibility and ethical behavior both on and off the court. She often shared with her players her 'Definite Dozen' which included the mandate *"take full responsibility."*[27]

Summitt was known to say that "you can't assume larger responsibility without taking responsibility for the small things, too . . . being responsible means making tough, unpopular decisions . . . admit to and make yourself accountable for mistakes—how can you improve if you're never wrong?"[28]

TRUST

When we think of trust, we think of people who are truthful and dependable. People who, when given a task to undertake (or when given privileged information), can be counted on to give their best to do the task right and see it through to completion. We think of people who will honor the privilege of information (shared with them) that is not for public consumption.

Trust is built on personal accountability and responsibility. And, trust is interactive. It involves two or more people interacting with each other and depending on each other for success. Galindo put it eloquently when she said, "no accountability, no trust."[29] Warren Bennis as dubbed by Forbes, a "Leader of Leaders," held that "the two most salient attributes of leaders are respect and trust" and also that "Leadership is about being present, and *trust lost is leadership lost.*"[30] Expanding his concept of trust, Bennis also said:

> I believe that trust is the underlying issue in not only getting people on your side, but having them stay there. There are four ingredients leaders have that generate and sustain trust:
>
> 1. *Constancy.* Whatever surprises leaders themselves may face, they don't create any for the group. Leaders are all of a piece; they stay the course.

2. *Congruity.* Leaders walk their talk. In true leaders, there is no gap between the theories they espouse and the life they practice.
3. *Reliability.* Leaders are there when it counts; they are ready to support their co-workers in the moments that matter.
4. *Integrity.* Leaders honor their commitments and promises.[31]

Mineo shared that "the foundation of a great workplace is created by organizational credibility, respect and fairness, which form the foundation of trust."[32] When a leader trusts and is trusted good things happen. But trust, like personal accountability, is built on judgment of actions and words over time. To positively affect judgment, one has to learn how to build trust, but both the learning and the process take time.

INTEGRITY

Integrity is the well-spring of trust. It is that flowing current of actions, inter-actions, and words (communication) done right that builds trust. Integrity is essential to a leader's credibility. According to Bennis, "Integrity simply means moral and intellectual honesty. Without it, we betray ourselves and others and cheapen every endeavor. Integrity is the single quality whose absence we feel most sharply on every level of our national life."[33]

In like fashion Carly Fiorina stated, "Leadership is about the integrity of one's character."[34] Integrity hinges on what a leader says and does. If a leader's words align with his/her actions and do so in every circumstance; that constancy and unwavering character speaks volumes to those in the organization. He/she is seen as a *standup person* who can be counted on. Donna E. Shalala, former US secretary of health and human services, sets forth "twelve lessons for managing a large public sector organization with honesty and integrity"—twelve lessons that are applicable to anyone working in public service or for the public good:

The buck starts here. In other words, standards must be set at the top.

Choose people based on both the content of their resume and their character.

The game is often won in the huddle. To put it another way, you need to foster interdisciplinary discussion.

Bureaucrat is not a four-letter word. It has been said that any society that respects its philosopher more than its plumbers will not have philosophies—or pipes—that hold water. Similarly, in trying to run an ethical organization, it would be foolish to overlook the opinions and abilities of the career public servant?

You have to be willing to not just hear the bad news but to listen to it.

Stop shoveling. The great Texas journalist Molly Ivins has written: "The first rule of holes is simple: When you are in one, stop digging." In other words, put the shovel down—do not dig deeper. If a mistake was made at HHS, we admitted it. And if senior appointee was accused of misconduct, we personally investigated the matter. We also made sure people understood that if they committed an error or a mistake—unless it was an ethical or legal issue—the department would rally around them.

You cannot cultivate honesty and integrity in the dark.

You cannot subordinate policy to politics.

You have to look at issues through a prism. Just as the images constantly change when a prism is turned, issues constantly change as the data or the circumstances or the political environment changes. That is why an issue must be looked at from every perspective, side, and viewpoint. At HHS, the executive secretariat provided the prism because it managed the enormous paper flow. It prepared a briefing book on every issue and policy.

It is your friends, not your enemies, who will often get you in trouble.

Ethical employers care about their employees.

If you don't tell people where you're going, you might end up somewhere else. In other words, you must have a vision, and you must share that vision.[35]

Shalala concludes that "to lead with integrity, you need to have the courage of your convictions."[36] Integrity demands that as an individual and as a leader, your words and actions reflect what you believe, and your integrity is based on what you believe. If you believe in *doing what is right* and do it with integrity, you will have great credibility.

SINCERITY

Like integrity, sincerity is a related to trust and via trust to credibility. When there is congruity between a leader's actions and his/her stated objectives sincerity is established. Referring back to Graham as a young man, a story is told of his need for employment as a young man.

Billy's father, having a few connections of his own, got Billy a job as a salesman with a hairbrush company. Both his father and his uncle shook their heads as Billy went off to sell hair brushes, both of them expecting him to be a flop. But Graham proved to be a natural and by the end of the summer "was the most successful salesman in two states."[37] It wasn't his convincing sales pitch or honest face that got him the title. Billy's passionate enthusiasm along with his genuine sincerity helped him achieve this near miraculous success.

When the opposite is true, sincerity and credibility diminish. The sense of the leader being sincere in what he/she believes, says, and does is tarnished, and his/her sincerity is lost or becomes highly questionable in the eyes of followers. Not a desirable outcome. However, sincerity like credibility in general, can be reestablished or regained but takes a proactive response to the situation that called the leader's sincerity into question.

In short, when an error has been made an apology can be given. However, as Basford holds, "All apologies are not created equal. While some apologies are perceived as quite heartfelt, others are appraised as insincere. These perceptions of apology sincerity matter, as research indicates that targets respond more positively to apologies that they consider sincere . . . In contrast, a leader whose apology is perceived to be insincere may engender negative follower reactions."[38]

Bashford further states that "in fact, when a leader's apology is appraised as insincere, it may do more harm than good."[39] So what's a leader to do? The answer is to work to insure that words and deeds are congruent; be humble and understand that questioning of your sincerity will come. What you have learned to do to reestablish your sincerity is what matters in the end, insuring that your words and actions are congruent.

CREDIBILITY AND LEADERSHIP

So, what is credibility, then, in terms of its impact on leadership? It is the difference between gaining followers and losing them. It is the difference between being able to assert influence and lacking the influence to affect a situation. It is the difference between having your vision for an organization accepted or rejected. It is the difference between being able to resolve a vital but disputed issue and having the issue left as a festering sore that will negatively impact an organization. It is the difference between being a successful leader and a leader who fails or is derailed.

Credibility is the defining and most significant soft skill characteristic of a leader. It is that element without which being a leader is impossible. Perhaps equally important, it is the essence upon which relationships are built and maintained. Credibility binds together the beliefs, words, and actions of an individual upon which that individual is judged personally and professionally. And, credibility enhances LSI.

Chapter 4

'Recalculating'

Leader Competence

Why is the term 'recalculating' utilized when we refer to leadership competence? To begin, all leaders need to retool or 'recalculate.' Doctors don't go to medical school and stop their education. They have to keep themselves abreast of the latest information for medicines, medical practice, and referrals. Likewise, biology teachers don't graduate with a bachelor's degree and know all the science they will need to teach over a career. As time moves forward, connections to learned materials and inventions and genetic engineering and the like change the biological implications from the past and for the future. All professions share the need for practitioners to remain up-to-date on the latest discoveries, innovations, and techniques for applying those to the tasks of their profession. As leaders, we need to set an example for the organization by working to improve our skillsets as the person in charge.

In the world of the GPS, if the driver varies from the route established, a familiar voice comes from the device with a commanding, 'recalculating . . . recalculating.' This in effect means that the GPS acknowledges the driver has gone astray and the GPS therefore tries to help the driver back onto the correct course. In an analogous way, if a leader is about to make a misstep, there should be a still, small voice within whispering 'recalculating . . . recalculating.' This of course, is the leader's conscience.

The competent person on a traverse, however, knows when they have purposefully ignored the information given to them via the GPS. Generally, they have done this because they have more or other information available. Of course, most of the time when the driver ignores route guidance, there is a reasonable rationale.

On occasion as one is traveling in the correct direction, there is a need to make a temporary change. Many times, that need takes the form of creature comforts—a restroom break, need to refuel, looking for a place to eat, and sometimes in the form of an emergency. So the route is changed due to necessity, but not without sacrifice of some sort. In this case, the sacrifice is not the route but another variable. Whenever a course is set, any deviation from that course comes at a cost. In this case, the additional expense comes in the form of time. As you know, when you enter a destination into a GPS, an estimated time of arrival (ETA) is given for the expectation of trip completion. As intended deviations are taken, that ETA moves further and further away.

Now in the case of competence, once your ETA is established and you share it with others, they will have an expectation about your arrival time. Those others might not notice if you are a few minutes late. But as you move further away from that ETA, the more concerned they will become. As a matter of fact, if this were someone you always checked in with before making a trip, your competence with that person (regarding ETA) might be in jeopardy. This would certainly be the case if you were late every time you visited them due to your decisions to vary from the prescribed course of time. So making adjustments to your route, even when necessary, can impact your arrival time, and in the case of a leader your perceived competence.

On the other hand, there are times that the GPS states "recalculating," and it is definitely the correct advice. How do you know the difference? If you have not intentionally varied from the scheduled course of travel, and you hear the words 'recalculating,' it is possible that you somehow missed an important piece of information. This can happen under many circumstances. You might have entered a very congested area of travel (a *lot* is going on in the organization under your direction), or when you are distracted by various other things, perhaps the music in the automobile is too loud. In an organization, there are times when we get so caught up in or preoccupied with the daily routine that we neglect to pay attention to our internal compass or GPS. Things are rolling along quite smoothly out on the open road, and then, all of a sudden we find ourselves in a very congested area of traffic.

At other times, the cause for error is less subtle. You are distracted by a huge storm, a baby crying, or the canine companion that is traveling with you just threw up in your lap. Likewise, in the organization, it may be smooth sailing when your boss falls and breaks a leg, or the city water must be shut down for three hours, or even worse, a shooter enters your building. Receiving the information 'recalculating' can happen in many instances, some are fairly minor and others are *major* events. Regardless, any recalculations come with a price. On occasion, the price is practically obsolete, and then for others, the cost could be career-changing. The important thing to bear in mind is that it is critical to heed the 'recalculation' warning and to refocus your attention quickly and get back on course.

Unfortunately, there is another occasion when the GPS may screech that dreaded word: 'recalculating.' This would come when you *think* you know more than the GPS and insist on going a different direction when, in fact, you are going the wrong way! If others are riding with you, they may begin to correct you and perhaps even implore you to change your direction. This is especially true if the area your misdirection has taken leads you into a dangerous situation. If this happens, your passengers will begin to lack trust in your ability to successfully guide them to the desired destination. Overconfidence can devastate competence. And, overconfidence is generally linked inversely to leadership talent and is often masked as charisma. Charisma, in and of itself, is generally a very positive attribute. However, many a leader has allowed charisma-based confidence based on feedback from others, and not their competence, to derail them.

Developing and maintaining competence in one's chosen field requires not only initial training but also continuous renewal. That is, once an aspiring leader has been immersed in the minutiae of his/her field, he/she must learn to apply what they have learned. Achieving competence represents a major career accomplishment: being able to function successfully at the highest level within your chosen field. Competence is more than a one-dimensional concept. It is the amalgamation of critical self-reflection and the perspective of others. For leaders, it is not only knowing that you have the requisite knowledge, skills, and ability to get the job done, it is having the respect and trust of those who you work with and who follow you as a leader. It is knowing what to do, how to do it, and knowing when and where to act or having the openness to input and learning that allows those actions. Leaders do not have to have all of the answers all of the time, but they do have to have ability to recognize the potential in any suggested course of action or idea that is proposed. They must be competent and have Leadership Intelligence (LSI).

In the LSI model, a clear separation is made between administrative/managerial 'hard' skill competencies such as expertise in financial management, use of technology, scheduling, or facility/grounds management. While these skills have value, being able to build a budget but lacking the ability to effectively communicate it to others and/or have others manage the budget once in place limits the effectiveness of having mastered the skill. Similarly, mastering the use of technology does little good for a leader who cannot utilize that technology to move the people in the organization toward its vision. True competence in effectively applying 'hard skills' requires mastery of 'soft skills'—that is, people-centered skills. Based on 'soft/people skills,' the LSI model addresses discernibility, perception, conflict resolution, problem solving and, decision making, planning and implementation, relationship building, and assessment and evaluation skills as composing the core 'soft skills' related to competence.

When we think of competence, we think of things like knowledge, work ethic, thoroughness, and drive. Those qualities come together in a man named Sam Walton.[1] Walton, the founder of the Wal-Mart chain, came from meager roots with his beginnings during the Great Depression. As a young boy, he took on jobs to help his family survive. At a very young age, Walton learned of determination and the value of a strong work ethic. Those early lessons imprinted Walton for the remainder of his life. Not only did he begin his work ethic early on, but he also was the youngest Eagle Scout in Missouri's history.

DISCERNIBILITY

A leader, to be effective, must have the skill of discernibility, including the ability to discern effective practices from ineffective practices. A leader is discernable when his/her beliefs, thoughts, ideas, words, and actions distinguish him/her from other leaders. The discernible leader is credible in the sense that his/her words and actions are congruent. He/she has displayed the type of ethical behavior, honesty, integrity, and responsibility that establish trust. Of leadership, Bolman and Deal say, "It is not tangible. It exists only in relationships and in the perception of the engaged parties."[2] Their description of leadership fits well with discernibility: it is in the perception and beliefs of peers and followers. And, those perceptions and beliefs are behaviorally based. They are dependent on what a leader does and says. In that sense, communication is especially significant with regard to leadership discernibility. A competent and secure leader's communication is easily distinguished from that of an insecure leader. As Jeff Boss, executive leadership coach, states, "insecurity is easily discernible through vocabulary. The words you choose and how you employ them determine how you're received—positively, negatively, influentially."[3] For his/her organization, the leader shows command of the knowledge and skills including the communication needed to succeed and applies that knowledge and those skills to affect the desired outcomes. For example, if a superintendent calls upon school personnel to consider moving from a standard six- or seven-period class schedule to a block schedule, school personnel expect the superintendent to have a sound working knowledge of block scheduling. They also expect that superintendent to possess the skills to help select and implement a block schedule that fits the individual schools within the district.

The other aspect of discernibility is that the leader must be able to distinguish work/practice that produces desired outcomes and work/practice that falls short. For example, a principal must be able to recognize good teaching when he/she sees it and in counterpoint must be able to recognize poor teaching when that is seen. More generally, a principal must be able to distinguish sound educational practices from unsound or questionable educational practices.

Furthermore, this skill is absolutely critical in aligning the right people. That is, a leader must be able discern the difference between those individuals who can be/are trusted advisors and those individuals whose advice tends to lead to bad situations. When knowledge of this nature and skills combine, such a leader has discernibility.

Consider the biblical account of Solomon, son of David, and King of Israel.[4] When the Lord Jehovah asked Solomon what he would desire above all else, Solomon did not request power or wealth. This man, who had been imprinted by his father (a man after God's own heart) requested wisdom. And so the story goes that two women both claiming to be the mother of a single child come to Solomon to settle their dispute. Because of his great discernibility, the wise king asks for a sword to cut the baby in two giving each mother half of the child.

Of course, the true mother of the child would willingly give the child away rather than to see it be killed. Thus, Solomon declared this woman to be the mother of the baby.

PERCEPTION

Perception is reality as the old saying goes. What we perceive to be real for us is real. Perception for a leader is dichotomous. It is how the leader is perceived by others both within and external to an organization. Leader perception is also how the leader perceives individuals within and external to the organization, the functioning of the organization, and the outcomes of organizational processes.

We all have a mental image of what an ideal leader should be and would do. And, while those images or perceptions of a leader vary as greatly as the number of followers of a leader, there are always commonalities. Gurr and Day in reporting the characteristics of successful school leaders based on the International Successful School Principalship Project (ISSPP) state, "A major understanding from 12 years of research in the ISSPP is that we can describe what successful school leadership looks like across the world."[5] They found that,

In summary, successful school leaders:

- have high expectations of all
- employ multiple conceptions of leadership (they are not wedded to the use of narrow concepts like instructional or transformational leadership) and utilise a core set of practices focused on setting direction, developing people, leading change and improving teaching and learning

- model leadership that is both heroic and inclusive
- foster collaboration and collective endeavor
- acknowledge and embrace their symbolic role
- display integrity, trust and transparency
- are people centered
- focus their efforts on the development of others
- are able to lead in challenging contexts and view challenges as obstacles to overcome rather than problems that are insurmountable
- develop a range of appropriate personal qualities, with appropriate core values and beliefs articulated and lived (such as a belief that all can learn).

Similar lists can be found describing successful business leaders. Peter Drucker[6] summarizing his observations made over a sixty-five-year consulting career said about the effective business executive was that what made them all effective is that they followed the same eight practices:

- They asked, "What needs to be done?"
- They asked, "What is right for the enterprise?"
- They developed action plans.
- They took responsibility for decisions.
- They took responsibility for communicating.
- They were focused on opportunities rather than problems.
- They ran productive meetings.
- They thought and said "we" rather than "I."

No single individual in all likelihood would meet all of the criteria listed by either Gurr and Day or Drucker. But human nature being what it is, the perception/expectation may be like the punch line in the joke circulating some years ago: a leader should either be able to walk on water or know where the rocks are. Leaders at times do tend to be perceived as taking on characteristics that are exceptional, but that is rarely, if ever, the reality. Perceptions of that nature are more often driven by a remarkable success fueled in large part by the leader's vision and knowledge and drive.

In discharging his/her daily responsibilities, a leader must be perceptive. He/she must have a clear perception of the ongoing activities both internal and external to the organization. He/she must be fully alert and aware of the circumstances and situation surrounding any given issue.

Returning to our opening remark about perception, what we perceive to be real, for us is real, it seems reasonable to say that if a leader wants to be perceived in a positive light he/she must do those things that create and maintain that perception as reality. He/she must be a knowledgeable, productive, caring but tough-minded individual. That same leader must develop perceptive skills that allow him/her to correctly judge people and events. Judgment skills can be learned and sharpened, but it is up to the leader to choose to do what is right often in the face of daunting circumstances. Making that choice will make perception reality.

CONFLICT RESOLUTION SKILLS

Conflict is a natural part of being human. Conflict generally begins with disagreement and then, if not resolved, escalates in conflict. Disagreement, of course, can be functional or dysfunctional. When disagreement leads to new thinking or innovative approaches, it is constructive or positive. When disagreement leads to disassociation or outright conflict, the results are most often bad.

Specifically, conflicts (problems) in organizations tend to arise from six sources, disputes, or concerns between or among individuals or groups involving: (1) people (professional interpersonal or group conflicts or in some instances intrapersonal conflicts); (2) tasks to be accomplished; (3) process issues; (4) resource allocation (fiscal, material, human, or informational resources); (5) product/outcome issues; and (6) pressure from internal or external sources.[7]

Unresolved conflicts in any one of these areas can be disruptive. To avoid those bad outcomes, a leader must have high-level conflict resolution skills. Bolman and Deal stress reframing conflicts to encourage all sides examine potential satisfactory solutions.[8]

Consider Mahatma Gandhi, who began his adult career as a lawyer but then committed his life to the pursuit of the independence of India. Gandhi did not accomplish this without personal sacrifice.[9] He was imprisoned on several occasions in his attempts at nonviolent transformation of the corrupt social and political systems of his time. Gandhi's accomplishments were not motivated by ambition. They were motivated by a desire to improve the conditions of his people and his quest for self-actualization.

As leaders, when we move to this place, understanding that what is best for others and the good of the organization, we will easily treat others with respect and consideration in resolving conflict. As we practice patience in dealing with the difficult to deal with, we will find conflict resolution to be a humanitarian effort, and as Gandhi would say, we will "become the change we would like to see in others."

Covey suggests a similar path based on his fourth habit. He spells out a conflict resolution approach that is beneficial to all individuals at odds and the organization as a whole. He encourages a win-win approach to conflict resolution:[10]

Think Win-Win isn't about being nice, nor is it a quick-fix technique. It is a character-based code for human interaction and collaboration.

Most of us learn to base our self-worth on comparisons and competition. We think about succeeding in terms of someone else failing—that is, if I win, you lose; or if you win, I lose. Life becomes a zero-sum game. There is only so much pie to go around, and if you get a big piece, there is less for me; it's not fair, and I'm going to make sure you don't get anymore. We all play the game, but how much fun is it really?

Win-Win sees life as a cooperative arena, not a competitive one. Win-Win is a frame of mind and heart that constantly seeks mutual benefit in all human interactions. Win-Win means agreements or solutions are mutually beneficial and satisfying. We both get to eat the pie, and it tastes pretty darn good!

Covey's thinking about conflict resolution is sound. But, as he succinctly says about Win-Win,

It is a balancing act between courage and consideration. To go for win-win, you not only have to be empathic, but you also have to be confident. You not only have to be considerate and sensitive, you also have to be brave. To do that—to achieve that balance between courage and consideration—is the essence of real maturity and is fundamental to win-win.[11]

It is also possible that the conflict either cannot be resolved win-win or cannot be resolved at all. In such instances, a leader must call upon his/her best judgment as to the correct course of action. An internalized GPS for applying leadership intelligence makes those decisions more palatable.

PROBLEM-SOLVING AND DECISION-MAKING SKILLS

The Great Depression in the United States began on October 29, 1929, a day known forever after as 'Black Tuesday,' when the American stock market—which had been roaring steadily upward for almost a decade—crashed, plunging the country into its most severe economic downturn yet.[12] Speculators lost their shirts; banks failed; the nation's money supply diminished; and companies went bankrupt and began to fire their workers in droves.

Meanwhile, President Herbert Hoover urged patience and self-reliance: He thought the crisis was just "a passing incident in our national lives," and that it wasn't the federal government's job to try to resolve. By 1932, one of the bleakest years of the Great Depression, at least one-quarter of the American workforce was unemployed. When President Franklin Roosevelt took office in 1933, he acted swiftly to try and stabilize the economy and provide jobs and relief to those who were suffering. Over the next eight years, the government instituted a series of experimental projects and programs, known collectively as the New Deal, which aimed to restore some measure of dignity and prosperity to many Americans. More than that, Roosevelt's New Deal permanently changed the federal government's relationship to the US populace.

Like conflict is a part of human nature, it is the nature of any enterprise that problems will arise. The problems may be small and relatively insignificant or rise to a level that threatens the existence of the organization. No matter where on the spectrum from minor to fatal a problem falls, it is incumbent upon an organizational leader to solve the problem in a timely, positive, productive manner. The solution must incorporate the best thinking not only of the leader but of organizational members (or, at times, those external to the organization) impacted by the decision.

The process employed here is reflective of both the reframing suggested by Bolman and Dean and Covey's win-win process. A leader must determine who should be involved in the decision-making process, proactively seek their input, and based upon available information arrive at the best decision. Of course, in some instances, the leader will have, perforce, to make unilateral decisions. Tannenbaum and Schmidt[13] in their classic *Harvard Business Review* article offer the following advice regarding involving others in decision making:

- If the subordinates have relatively high needs for independence. (As we all know; people differ greatly in the amount of direction that they desire.)
- If the subordinates have a readiness to assume responsibility for decision making. (Some see additional responsibility as a tribute to their ability; others see it as "passing the buck.")
- If they have a relatively high tolerance for ambiguity. [Some employees prefer to have clear-cut directives given to them; others prefer a wider area of freedom.)
- If they are interested in the problem and feel that it is important.
- If they understand and identify with the goals of the organization.
- If they have the necessary knowledge and experience to deal with the problem,
- If they have learned to expect to share in decision making. (Persons who have come to expect strong leadership and are then suddenly confronted with the request to share more fully in decision making are often upset by this new experience. On the other hand, persons who have enjoyed a considerable amount of freedom resent the boss who begins to make all the decisions himself.)

It is in determining whether to involve others or to what extent to involve others that an internalized GPS based on LSI can be beneficial. It can help the leader identify the contextual clues that guide the decision-making process and the final decision.

RELATIONSHIP BUILDING

In discussing credibility, we shared that credibility is the essence upon which relationships in are built and maintained. That straightforward statement captures the vital importance of relationships to leader success. Leadership is a social process. That process plays out within an organization and as a part of the interface between an organization and individuals and entities external to the organization. Without the ability to build and maintain working relationships, a leader is doomed to failure: as the poet John Donne said, "no man is an island unto himself."

A leader must work in cooperation and coordination with others to achieve organizational success and through organizational success, success for himself/herself and members of the organization. Reina and Reina say, "It is people working in relationship with one another that ultimately delivers results."[14]

Relationship building within an organization for a leader begins with his/her openness to others and the development of trust. As related by Reina and Reina:

> At the core of trust building is increasing our awareness of ourselves and our behaviors with others. Through our heightened awareness, we are in a stronger position to choose to practice behaviors that build trust. By practicing these behaviors consistently, leaders earn their trustworthiness.

Trust is reciprocal; you have to give it to get it, and it is built step-by-step over time. A common mistake leaders make is to assume that their position, role, or title earns them their trustworthiness. Nothing could be further from the truth. The only thing that earns a leader trustworthiness is the way they behave. And to be trusted by others, leaders must first be willing to trust them. Trust begets trust.

Leaders earn trustworthiness by practicing such behaviors as honoring their agreements; behaving consistently, even during challenging times; investing in people by providing feedback and opportunities to learn new skills; acknowledging employees' capabilities by including them in decisions, even the big ones; by maintaining open channels of communication; and yes, by holding people accountable.

Trustworthy leaders are safe—safe to talk to, to share problems with, and to share fears and concerns with. They are safe to be human with. As a result, people are safe to challenge the system and perform beyond expectations. Employees feel more freedom to express their creative ideas. They are more willing to take risks, admit mistakes, and learn from those mistakes.[15]

One of the great relationship builders of current day can be found in William Jefferson "Bill" Clinton, former US president. Clinton had an uncanny ability to make everyone he met feel like the most important person in the room.[16] A great deal of this ability appears to have been imprinted into the core of his personality. However, because relationship building was/is so important to Clinton, he invested time into becoming even better at it. As a matter of fact, during his career, at the end of each day, he would take a 3 × 5 notecard to write notes about each new person he met. He did this in the event he might meet that person again, he would refresh his memory about that person by reviewing his notecard. It is stated that he had amassed over 10,000 of these notecards by 1980.

Once a bond of trust has been established, it must be maintained. Reina and Reina suggest three areas where trust must be built and maintained: contractual trust, communication trust, and competence trust. They relate about each area, respectively:

> Contractual trust involves managing expectations, establishing boundaries, delegating appropriately, encouraging mutually serving intentions, keeping agreements, and being congruent in our behavior. How we practice these behaviors demonstrates the quality of our character as perceived by ourselves and others.
> Communication trust is the willingness to share information, tell the truth, admit mistakes, maintain confidentiality, give and receive constructive feedback, and speak with good purpose. How we practice these behaviors demonstrates our willingness to disclose and the quality of that disclosure.
> Competence trust involves acknowledging people's skills and abilities, allowing people to make decisions, involving others and seeking their input, and helping people learn skills. How we practice these behaviors demonstrates our willingness to trust our capability and that of others.[17]

With a trusting relationship well established within an organization, a leader can move forward with planning and implementing the steps to be undertaken to move toward accomplishing the mission and goals of the organization. He/she can also move toward establishing the same bond of trust with individuals and entities external to an organization. In practice, a leader is probably working in both arenas simultaneously.

Building external relationship, like building internal relationships, is dependent primarily on establishing trust. A good place to start is with honesty and candor. As Goldsmith shared in regard to analyst and shareholder relations but equally applicable to any stakeholder, constituent, or customer with an interest in a specific organization, "Provide honest—and even conservative—business-performance projections."[18]

Beyond honesty, the next step is to be proactive. Reach out to stakeholders, constituents, community members, and organizations. They all want to know about an important organization in their community. And, where possible, establish individual relationships. They pay long-term dividends both personally (there are a lot of very interesting people out there that make life better just by knowing them) and for the organization.

Well-honed LSI can help steer you in establishing work as well as external relationships. It can guide you to the people and places that add meaning to what you do professionally and personally. It can enhance your ability to establish productive and long-lasting trusting relationships.

PLANNING AND IMPLEMENTATION SKILLS

In chapter 6, we will discuss leadership vision, but we mention it here as an introduction to planning and implementation. Suffice it to say here that vision without planning and implementation skills is a hollow vessel. Skills in planning and implementation allow a leader to facilitate his/her vision for the organization. Chief among planning and implementation skills is the ability to bring together and motivate individuals and groups. In any organization, it is the individual and group interaction of the work that produce desired outcomes. A second necessary skill is the ability to focus the work of those individuals and groups on the desired outcomes of the organization. A third skill is the ability to gain consensus. And, a final skillset is the ability to objectively assess and evaluate the impact that has been planned and implemented.

ASSESSMENT AND EVALUATION

A wise, experienced school administrator once said that you should know people for what they are and treat with them accordingly. The latter part of this statement seems a pejorative but that was not the intention. He meant only that every individual has a unique interaction with a leader. And, further, that to get the most (he meant the highest level of performance) out of an individual a leader must not only know them well but also know what motivates them. Said another way, a leader must be capable of assessing and evaluating the strengths and weaknesses of each individual with whom he/she works. A leader must also be able to assess and evaluate the intricacies of the social/political interactions within the organization and, at times, the interaction of the organizational members with individuals or entities external to the organization. And finally, a leader must be able to assess and evaluate the task processes that lead to the desired outcomes of the organization.

COMPETENCE AND LEADERSHIP

Competence is to credibility as the keystone is to a masonry arch. With a solid keystone, the arch holds solidly and will fail only if the surrounding structure is damaged or the strength of the structure eroded over time. Competence is the keystone that allows a leader to bind, and over time, hold the organization together by not only properly carrying out the hard skills/ tasks of his/her job but by also successfully applying the essential soft skills concomitant with the hard skill tasks. Only when organizational members believe a leader is competent can the leader truly be said to have credibility. A leader with high LSI has a greater probability of establishing through his/her actions that he/she is competent and therefore enhances his/her credibility.

Chapter 5

'Lost Satellite Reception'

Leader Inspiration

Occasionally when traveling, you get to an area that is completely unrecognized by your GPS. Or perhaps it's a very cloudy day and your GPS cannot receive signals to give you directions. Or something more exotic may be happening. 'Space weather' can occur when there is a strong solar storm, or someone may be using an illegal jamming device, or interference from a close-by adjacent band transmitter may be occurring.[1]

As GPS devices are used, data is gathered which helps them acquire satellites quickly at the start of each use. If a device is used daily, it should be able to acquire satellites in a minute or less. Using a GPS device while it is outdoors with a clear view of the entire sky is the ideal condition for acquiring satellites.

At the time when it is not working so quickly, perhaps it just needs a little inspiration. It could be that this is the first time it has been asked to perform. It would be completely understandable for it to take a wee bit longer to get the inspiration to start humming. Conceivably, it might not be responsive to directions if it is improperly positioned or has been inactive for a while. Many of us need a warm cup of coffee to inspire us to move forward in the to start the day as well.

Sometimes when new maps are loaded (or the GPS has had a master reset), it is slower to respond. Similarly changes to policy, procedures, and protocol make the leader a little less certain when making decisions. On occasion the leader must take a few minutes to think through the new directives to be certain they are conforming to new standards.

Finally, if a device has been over five hundred miles without being utilized, it can be a bit slow to respond to your instructions. Similarly, the old adage 'if you don't use it, you lose it' applies. A few stretches and practice swings will inspire a golfer to head to the course. Similarly, and almost without exception,

49

beginning a new route requires inspiration. Sometimes the inspiration that is needed is small, other times a bit larger. But the time invested in 'inspiration' can reap huge benefits.

The Leadership Intelligence (LSI) concept identifies inspirational leaders as those who galvanize an organization to action, leading to individual and organizational success. Many times inspirational leaders are charismatic. However, charisma is not a prerequisite for the inspirational leader. As Baldoni stated, "Charisma enhances one's presence but it is not essential."[2] Peter Drucker in discussing effective executives and charisma shared that, "Harry Truman did not have one ounce of charisma . . . yet he was among the most effective chief executives in U.S. history."[3]

In this same vein, Baldoni related:

> While inspirational leaders are often charismatic, as were John Kennedy and Ronald Reagan, leadership inspiration comes more from the power of possibilities. Bill Gates is an exemplar. Gates does not warm to the spotlight the way celebrities do. It is the power of his ideas, first at Microsoft and now at the Bill and Melinda Gates Foundation. His inspiration draws bright capable people to him the way moths are drawn to flames.[4]

Another moving leader, Martin Luther King Jr., is one of the first names that comes to mind when we think of being inspired.[5] Although King's lifetime mission was to improve the quality of life, as well as justice for his contemporaries, he did not always intend to do it via means of the pulpit. Initially, King believed the best way to exact change would be as an advocate of peace through the justice system as an attorney.

Having been reared in the church, he mused over that platform being used as a vehicle for nonviolent inspiration of the civil rights movement. Over time, he determined that it could, and inspire he did. The final years of his highly charismatic and short life were spent inspiring those around him to reach for a more equal and just society.

In reality, a majority of leaders are not charismatic but attempt to inspire individuals within the organization through words and deeds. They attempt to put the individuals who make up the organization (and through them the organization itself) in the best position to succeed. At the height of the recent economic down turn, a time when leadership was often in question, Baldoni held:

> Needed in this downturn are men and women who can inspire, not simply with the power of their personality but with the power of their imagination. Such vision need not be reserved solely for those at the top of the pyramid; rather it can be recognized and nurtured by those who are in position to groom and promote the next generation of leaders. Here are three attributes to look for.

Realism. Inspirational leaders are rooted in reality. They know the facts but remain undeterred. This sense separates them from fools who are quick to rush into things before considering consequences. Inspirational leaders are keenly aware of what could go wrong and are honest about it. It is this honesty that draws capable contributors. They sense the leader knows the facts but is willing to experiment as well as persevere.

Improvement. Wanting to make things better is essential to inspiration. Therefore, inspirational leaders value innovations. They are inherently creative because they are not satisfied with the status quo. Very importantly they seek to open doors for people who can innovate in their function, be it product development or logistics. They encourage employees to think for themselves.

Optimism. You must believe in the better tomorrow. This is easy to do when the economy is rising but more difficult when it is shrinking. Optimism for the inspirational leader is not merely inherent; it is contagious. Others feel it and want to feed off it. This is essential to getting the work done now and developing next generation initiatives that will position the organization for success over the long term.[6]

Wilson and Rice, addressing inspirational leadership "in times of adversity," share:

Inspirational leadership can breathe the capacity for responding to adversity into the heart and soul of an organization, and this capacity becomes part of the organization's culture. If people are involved in building and accomplishing the inspirational leader's vision for the organization, if their work is connected to that vision and to their own motivations and values, the value of the resulting commitment to the overall success of the organization cannot be overstated. If the organization's culture is one that inspires rather than oppresses, it can only have the effect of creating a more productive organization and profitable bottom line.[7]

From a North American perspective, inspirational leadership blends the *charismatic*, *transformational*, and *value-based* styles of leading:

- Charismatic leaders bring unique gifts to their organization. They are visionary and have a highly developed sense of strategic timing. They are unconventional and willing to take calculated risks.
- Transformational leaders develop special relationships with their followers. They challenge the status quo and pay attention to their followers' desires to find meaning in work and for personal development.
- Value-based leaders make the daily work of their followers more meaningful. They help their organizations develop an appealing vision of what lies in the future and generate confidence that the vision can be achieved.

But difficult times are not the sole realm for the emergence or need for inspirational leaders. Inspirational leaders are needed in good times as much as in bad times and in fact may act like a deterrent from hardship. In *Catalyzing Inspirational Leadership: Approaches and Metrics for Twenty-First-Century Executives*, Seidman offers these suggestions for leaders willing to take the "journey to inspirational leadership" that will improve performance for individuals and organizations:

> *Rethink fundamentals.* Everybody knows changing culture is important, but we tend to approach it in an ad hoc fashion. Authentically understanding, shaping, and leveraging your culture will differentiate your organization in the marketplace and drive sustainable growth and impact.
>
> *Focus on a higher purpose.* Purpose is enduring. It connects your actions to significance. Purpose makes businesses sustainable.
>
> *Give trust away.* Trust begets trust. Employees who feel truly trusted are less likely to betray that trust because they understand innately that it works to their benefit.
>
> *Scale values and get deliberate with culture.* Many companies are deeply stuck. They understand instinctively that the financial and environmental crises of our time require new behaviors. They're just beginning to take the journey. But to be activated, individuals must personally commit to changing how they think, how they decide, and how they behave.
>
> *Embrace transparency.* There are no more secrets. This is a twenty-first-century reality. If your actions don't match your words, your reputation and bottom line will suffer.[8]

These same practices/ideas hold true for the inspirational leader's interaction with individuals and entities external to the organization. They inspire belief and faith in the organization, it goals and purposes, and move those external individuals and entities to support the individuals within the organization and through them the organization itself.

These leaders encourage individuals to grow professionally and personally and provide the resources to promote that growth process. They are passionate, enthusiastic about what they do. They come across as genuine. They are unrelenting optimists and bring seemingly boundless energy to what they do. Put simply, they inspire by being themselves.

ENTHUSIASTIC

Like many of the characteristics related to LSI, being enthusiastic has a dual nature. For a leader to be enthusiastic he/she must have, display, and communicate enthusiasm individually toward the work of his/her organization including his/her role in the organization. He/she must be well grounded and have a firm grasp of their individual beliefs.

Hundreds to thousands of aspiring young science teachers were thus motivated by Christa McAuliffe. Her enthusiasm and energy to become the first teacher in space encouraged many to follow in her footsteps to become science teachers and women leaders of all types.[9] Of the initial 1,100 teacher applicants for the opportunity to go up in space, McAuliffe was selected for the position. According to NASA official Alan Ladwig, "she had an infectious enthusiasm," and it was further reported by Mark Travis of the *Concord Monitor* that it "was her manner that set her apart from the other candidates."

A leader must also be capable of generating enthusiasm in organizational members. In their discussion of inspirational leaders, Zenger and Folkman list one type as *"Enthusiasts."*[10] They show passion, vitality, and vigor. Passive behaviors evade them and dynamic decisions are naturally made. They are extroverts who generate energy and excitement. Enthusiasts breathe life into organizations. The companion behavior is *making an emotional connection.*

It is impossible for a leader to inspire without being enthusiastic. A leader's enthusiasm must not be over-the-top unbounded enthusiasm, but enthusiasm that is focused, directed, and engages peers and followers. Or as Glassman and Bruce shared, enthusiasm "can be thought of as an ardent zeal toward a project or goal."[11] Enthusiasm speaks to the personal interest of a leader, to the interest he/she has in his/her organization, and the work of the organization.

Moreover, enthusiasm speaks to the effort a leader expends with and on behalf of the members of the organization to insure the quality of the product produced. As Russell stated, "Enthusiasm for work is a precious commodity. Because work is such a central component of all our lives and enthusiasm appears to support enhanced productivity, it behooves us to thoughtfully promote enthusiasm and engagement through work."[12]

Inspiring enthusiasm in others requires knowing others as well as they know themselves. As George related, "In order for leaders to generate and maintain excitement and enthusiasm, they must be able to appraise how their followers feel, and be knowledgeable about how to influence these feelings."[13] What George sets out is a daunting task but one that a leader with high levels of emotional intelligence can manage. He says:

> Effective leaders need to be able to distinguish between, for example, excitement and enthusiasm that are faked versus excitement and enthusiasm that are genuinely felt. When excitement and enthusiasm are faked, a leader needs to determine why as well as try to instill real feelings of excitement and enthusiasm. Through their ability to appraise other people's emotions, their knowledge of emotions, and their ability to manage emotions, leaders who are high on emotional intelligence are likely to be better able to decipher when expressed emotions are genuine, understand why they may be faked, and influence followers

to experience genuine excitement, enthusiasm, confidence and optimism rather than these fake feelings.[14]

Touching on both points, individual enthusiasm and transference of enthusiasm to others, Russell, in a qualitative study of educational leaders, found:

> The information gathered leads to the conclusion that enthusiasm and engagement with work is related to a collaborative leadership style, a strong work ethic, and alignment of personal and organizational missions. That is, educational leaders who (1) seek to achieve progress through collaboration, (2) exhibit a strong work ethic, and (3) clarify for themselves and others how the organizational mission aligns with personal mission are more likely, themselves, to be engaged and enthusiastic, while also promoting the same characteristics among those with whom they work.[15]

Of course, no one can be enthusiastic twenty-four/seven but resourceful leaders find a way to project enthusiasm a predominant amount of time. Even when relaxed, these leaders can summon enthusiasm and passion for a topic of interest when called upon. On those occasions, a leader calls upon his/her energy to enhance his/her enthusiasm.

ENERGETIC

One could say that energy or being energetic is the catalyst that ignites enthusiasm. Imagine doing anything that you enjoy tremendously including work and then try to imagine that doing the same thing with no emotion or energy. The scenario takes a decidedly sad turn. Those sad outcomes can be avoided if leaders apply their energy wisely. Their energy must be utilized to drive fulfilling the mission of the organization. And, they must be mindful that while energy is renewable, it is not infinite. As with enthusiasm energy needs to be focused, directed, and applied in such a fashion as to engage peers and followers. A leader must be energetic and should generate energy in others. Patterson and Kelleher wrote, "Energy is essential to effective leadership. In your role, you not only need to stay personally energized but also must energize others."[16] Loeher and Schwartz hold that there are types of energy, "physical, emotional, mental and spiritual" and posit four principles for fully engaging your energy:

THE 4 PRINCIPLES OF FULL ENGAGEMENT

Principle 1: Full engagement requires drawing on four separate but related sources of energy: physical, emotional, mental and spiritual.

Principle 2: Because energy diminishes both with overuse and with underuse, we must balance energy expenditure with intermittent energy renewal.

Principle 3: To build capacity we must push beyond our normal limits, training in the same systematic way that elite athletes do.

Principle 4: Positive energy rituals—highly specific routines for managing energy are the key to full engagement and sustained high performance.[17]

For a leader to be perceived as being energetic, he/she must be energetic. Patterson and Kelleher said it well:

To be an effective leader, you must use positive energy to communicate effectively and empathetically with those you lead, to nurture their self-efficacy, to support their growth and ability to respond to workplace challenges. The need for you to have reserves of positive energy is especially acute during periods of intense stress, when the organization faces the threat of storms. One of your key roles is to enable followers to transform the negative emotional response (e.g., fear that the threat may generate) into the positive emotional responses (e.g., excitement at a new opportunity) that create the full engagement of high performance. As you will see in the next chapter, experienced and effective school leaders demonstrate strategies for enabling this transformation.[18]

PASSIONATE

Leaders who believe in what they are doing are passionate. Passion for what you do arises from the desire to do what you undertake well, to pursue perfection and success at the highest levels. Passion is the sustaining element that allows the inspirational leader to have an ongoing thirst for success and to inspire passion for the organization's work within organizational members. Without passion, energy is soon expended and enthusiasm dwindles. In their book, *Passion & Purpose: Stories from the Best and Brightest Young Business Leaders,* Coleman et al. hold that "Young business people want to find purpose in their profession and have a passion for what they do."[19] As Love shared regarding business executives, "Through their passions, these leaders impact the workforce in a way that delivers both business results and individual fulfillment." This is about more than skills and competencies. Passions are the deep internal drivers of behavior that distinguish good leaders from great ones. In the final analysis, for a leader to ignite passion in others, they must be passionate themselves.[20] Love describes 10 archetypes of passion and states that "Each of the 10 Passion Archetypes is present to some degree in all of us." Moreover, that "passions also determine how you might influence the generation and utilization of knowledge in the organization or on a team that you're leading."[21]

The Creator: The archetype of beauty and aesthetics, the Creator focuses on translating mental concepts into forms or representations that can be shared with others. The goal of the Creator's work is to touch others emotionally. Creators are the vessels from which true art emerges.

The Conceiver: Conceivers are passionate strategists who avidly dissect plans, concepts, or information to develop a more extensive comprehension of their underlying complexities. Individuals with this archetype are powerful "idea junkies" who thrive in the exploration of multifaceted concepts and assimilate them so rapidly that others struggle to keep up. In an organization seeking innovation, Conceivers are a valuable asset.

The Discoverer: An archetype that thrives in exploration, Discoverers are the truth seekers of the organization. They relentlessly focus on a hypothesis and will work tirelessly to determine its accuracy. Consumed with finding the information they seek; some Discoverers can focus on little else until it is obtained.

The Processor: Processors are the practical minded sustainers of structure, function, and tradition in the organization. They are highly analytic and enjoy sifting through data to determine what it reveals. They are gifted at utilizing information and data to identify unseen landmines that the organization might encounter in the future.

The Teacher: These are the knowledge exchanger and mentors of the organization who enjoy taking others under their wing. For the Teacher, the focus is on both sharing information and learning from the insights of others who assimilate that information. Teachers play an essential role in growing and retaining organizational knowledge.

The Connector: Avid relationship nurturers and negotiators, Connectors are the bridge builders of the organization. They are gifted networkers, good listeners, and adept communicators who are passionate about interfacing with others to seek common ground from which to work.

The Healer: As the clinicians of the organization, Healers are the first to notice pain or dysfunction on a team or within the organization at large and take personal responsibility for eradicating it. Healers work selflessly to assist others with navigating through painful or difficult situations and contribute significantly behind the scenes to create a work culture that supports thriving.

The Altruist: As the moral compass of the organization, the Altruist will challenge the team to achieve goals while contributing to society as a whole. With a focus that is balanced between internal objectives and community needs, the Altruist is an archetype of social conscience.

The Transformer: "If it ain't broke, fix it anyway" might be the mantra of this archetype. Transformers gravitate toward change and chaos and thrive in finding the new order that will emerge. They demonstrate a strong comfort with ambiguity and an avid sense of adventure.

The Builder: Builders are the architects of the organization who boldly take on seemingly insurmountable challenges. They enjoy designing the blueprint for the organization and making it a reality. Builders are masters at constructing new businesses or organizations in previously uncharted territories. Courage, risk taking, and a need for freedom are hallmarks of this archetype.

Love concludes by saying, "As a leader, it's not sufficient to merely understand the passions that drive you or your staff. You must also master the application of passion-driven strengths and carefully manage the vulnerabilities to which someone with your passions might succumb."[22]

Speaking about passion in relation to school leadership, Davies and Brighouse state that, "Passionate leadership is about energy, commitment, a belief that every child can learn and will learn, a concern with social justice and the optimism that we can make a difference. It takes leadership from the realm of a role or a job to one of an abiding drive to enhance childrens' learning and childrens' lives."[23] Further, Davies and Brighouse articulate seven things that passionate educational leaders do:

First, passionate leaders articulate the vision. Passionate leadership is about a deep-rooted belief in better opportunities and alternative outcomes. The ability to conceptualise those new futures and communicate them in a clear and concise way is vital. A vision should connect to the reality of the individuals in the organisation's current experience as well as the hope and aspirations for the future. In essence it has to connect to the heart as well as the head. The ability also to convey both the sense of importance and urgency of the journey to new and better futures is critical. It will only happen of course, if others have faith and trust that the leader can achieve the change and that all those in the organisation are involved in this process and its outcomes so they can commit to the vision.

Second, passionate leaders share the values. They move beyond the vision and mission statements and not only articulate values in written statements and programmes but also in their everyday speech and interactions. Invitational leadership highlights how each and every person is valuable and important. In the educational publishing world, we are immensely saddened by the series of books entitled *Getting the Buggers to:* . . . *'learn'* . . . *'do their home work'* . . . *'read'* and so on. Is that how we think of children? Are they not unique creations with individual capabilities How passionate leaders talk about children, colleagues and the school demonstrate their deep-seated values. How values are expressed and lived in day-to-day speech is vital if passionate leaders are to create a shared sense of moral purpose.

Third, passionate leaders set examples and standards that are possible. They convince people, by their personal standards, of what can be achieved and they behave ethically. They set clear goals that are achievable and encourage students and staff to meet them. They move beyond glib sayings such as 'raising the bar and narrowing the gap.' This year, standing outside the Olympic museum in Lausanne, one of us walked under the men's high jump bar (set at the record height)—he certainly could not jump it and raising it would not be an incentive to try! So what are achievable and meaningful success criteria? Setting targets so that 85 per cent of our children can be above average shows little understanding of the mathematical concept of average! Better that 100 per cent of our children can achieve their individual learning targets.

Fourth, passionate leaders are committed for the long term. They build in sustainable approaches to learning and organisational development. They have a belief system that all children can achieve and that all children will achieve. Data is a key factor here. We would prefer the expression 'data-informed' to 'data-driven'. Data-driven suggests that we react to short-term numerical results and bend all our efforts in that direction. Data-informed means we use quantitative data as indicative information but also balance it with qualitative insights about a child's many talents. Information and judgment are necessary to build a holistic picture of a child's progress in order to develop strategies and approaches to enhance deep learning.

Fifth, passionate leaders care. They care in a positive way—'care to make a difference' and 'care to challenge'. They care for the person and support pupils' teachers and parents in their roles as individuals and in their educational roles. Care can be considered as 'soft' and 'easy going' but real care both looks after the person as an individual and challenges their performance, attitude and commitment. Moving from a comfortable and adequate environment to one of high achievement and challenge often involves personal and professional challenge. That takes courage not to accept the *status quo*. Moving from a 'cruising' or 'strolling' school to a high-achieving school can be as difficult a journey as moving from failure to satisfactory.

Thus passionate leaders are courageous leaders, because they have the courage to challenge. This is a major factor in turning passion into action.

Sixth, passionate leaders celebrate. They celebrate achievements and success in the broadest sense. How individuals learn, socialise, contribute to society and make moral judgments are all areas for celebration and recognition. Believing that learning and education is hard work as well as enjoyable and fun is part of the positive outlook they develop. The culture of the school should be bringing out the best in everyone and celebrating when we do so. Passionate leaders create ceremonies and traditions as formal means of celebration. Most significantly in their daily acts of recognition and kindness they celebrate their colleagues' and students' achievements. How we engage in the learning journey as a process of commitment and passion should be a major reason for celebration and success.

Finally, passionate leaders are driven because it matters—it matters to them that they make a difference![24]

Whether in the private or public sector, passion is an asset for the inspirational leader. In combination with enthusiasm and energy, passion allows him/

her to remain invigorated about the work to be done. Passion also enhances a leader's ability to dampen or withstand those moments/times when the path is not clear or the results not as desired. It sees him/her through.

OPTIMISTIC

Optimism is yet another dimension of inspiration that tends to drive success. Optimism is based on the belief that actions and outcomes will have positive effect/impact. No difficult situation is impossible to rectify. If, as a leader, you are not optimistic, it is difficult, if not impossible, to convince others of the worth of a decision/action or the shared purpose articulated in the mission/ vision statement of a business or school.

Winston Churchill was once quoted as saying, "optimists see opportunities in every difficulty."[25] Yet regardless of his optimism, Churchill was faced with many skeptics. He was prime minister when Hitler was persecuting the Jews, and all of the area was frozen in disbelief. Disbelief in what was happening and disbelief that they could make a change. Ever the optimist, though, Churchill single-handedly turned around public opinion with a series of optimistic messages. In just a few weeks, he had convinced the masses that in warring with Germany, they could surely win.

Optimism is like the butterfly effect based on the work of Lorenz. The butterfly effect is the concept from chaos theory that the smallest change, even the mere flap of a butterfly's wings, can have profound consequences, such as generating a tornado on the other side of the world. Optimism likewise, even in small amounts, can create change but in a positive manner, if not overdone. As Wiseman shared, "When you play the role of the optimist, you may undervalue the struggle the team is experiencing or their hard-fought learning and work (or give the impression that you do). Your staff may wonder if you have lost your tether to reality."[26]

It is in remaining realistic that leaders are best able to utilize their optimism. Menkes related that based on his research he had "turned up three essential capabilities that allow leaders in today's turbulent world not only to perform at their best, but also to get the best out of their people." He describes these capabilities as 'catalysts' to successful leadership. The first of these catalysts is realistic optimism, about which he says:

> *Realistic optimism:* people with this trait possess confidence without self-delusion or irrationality. These people pursue audacious goals, which others would typically view as impossible pipedreams, while at the same time remaining aware of the magnitude of the challenges confronting them and the difficulties that lie ahead.[27]

When a leader presents himself/herself as passionate about his/her work, the work of others, and the organization as a whole, he/she creates an atmosphere in which the probability of positive outcomes is enhanced. The leader and members of the organization have taken possession of the organization and its purposes with all the positive potential that entails. They believe in what they are doing and have committed to it.

Ronald W. Reagan was described by his contemporaries as one of the most optimistic Americans ever known. He had a mindset for success and was designated the 'great communicator.' Colin Powell served under Reagan and said "optimism was the secret behind Reagan's charisma."[28]

GENUINE

Genuineness is the most significant consideration in relation to inspirational leadership. Enthusiasm, energy, passion, optimism, and courage play vital roles. They fire the *esprit de corps* and light the way for success. But, unless a leader is clearly perceived as being genuine, having a genuine interest in the success of the individuals that make up an organization, and vested in the success of the organization itself, as opposed to simply seeking to serve his/her own best interests and that path to success, it is unlikely that he/she will be seen as genuine.

To truly inspire, people must believe that what the leader says and does is based on genuine, real, authentic concern. That type of concern inspires. As MacFarland said so eloquently, "Genuine (authentic) leadership impresses and inspires, and this is the heart of true leadership that influences successful and sustained positive changes in individuals, groups, and organizations."[29] Goffee and Jones held that, "Employees will not follow a CEO who invests little of himself in his leadership behaviors. People want to be led by someone 'real.'"[30] But as with most leadership characteristics, genuine or authentic behaviors, comes with a cautionary caveat. Gruenfeld and Zander state:

> We'd rather be—or follow—a leader who is for real than one who is faking it. Acting in a way that feels truthful, candid, and connected to who you really are is important, and is a leadership quality worth aspiring to.
>
> On the other hand, being who you are and saying what you think can be highly problematic if the real you is a jerk. In practice, we've observed that placing value on being authentic has become an excuse for bad behavior among executives. It's important to realize that what makes you is not just the good stuff—your values, aspirations and dreams; the qualities others love most. For most people, what comes naturally can also get pretty nasty. When you are overly critical, non-communicative, crass, judgmental, or rigid, you are

probably at your most real—but you are not at your best. In fact, it is often these most authentic parts of a leader that need the most management.[31]

Warrell suggests five ways that leaders can 'unlock' authentic leadership:

Share authentically—Unlock the power of vulnerability.
Unlock the power of individuality.
Listen authentically—Unlock the power of presence.
Acknowledge authentically—Unlock the power of appreciation.
Serve authentically—Unlock the power of other-centeredness.[32]

Real, authentic, or genuine leaders, as Gruenfield and Zander point out, manage their authenticity.[33] They insure that their actions are congruent with their words. They act in such ways as to generate respect, trust, and a sense of genuineness. They inspire because they put their best foot forward and lead with character and dignity. They have that inner compass that guides them to the proper action or words.

COURAGEOUS

In all organizations, there will be times when courage is needed to face difficult and trying situations/times. Inspirational leaders have the courage to face dilemmas head on when strengthened by their belief in themselves and the organization. They call upon their inner compass to guide them to the proper decisions/actions. They are unafraid to admit errors and to take proper corrective action if that is what is called for. They are courageous.

But where does that courage come from? Reardon believes that while courage can be spontaneous it is more often a learned skill. She reports:

> Through interviews with more than 200 senior and midlevel managers who have acted courageously—whether on behalf of society, their companies, their colleagues, or their own careers—I've learned that this kind of courage is rarely impulsive. Nor does it emerge from nowhere.
>
> In business, courageous action is really a special kind of calculated risk taking. People who become good leaders have a greater than average willingness to make bold moves, but they strengthen their chances of success—and avoid career suicide—through careful deliberation and preparation. Business courage is not so much a visionary leader's inborn characteristic as a skill acquired through decision-making processes that improve with practice. In other words, most great business leaders teach themselves to make high-risk decisions. They learn to do this well over a period of time, often decades.[34]

She concludes in assessing the learning of courage as skills that:

> In the end, courage in business rests on priorities that serve a personal, an organizational, or a societal philosophy. When this philosophy is buttressed by clear, obtainable primary and secondary goals, an evaluation of their importance, a favorable power base, a careful assessment of risks versus benefits, appropriate timing, and well-developed contingency plans, managers are better empowered to make bold moves that serve their organizations, their careers, and their own sense of personal worth.[35]

Returning to the theme from our discussion of competence, courage is also about doing 'what is right.' It is not choosing the safe path or the path of least resistance. It is the fortitude to hold yourself accountable for all that you say and do. Ford Walston posits twelve behaviors of a courageous leader:

> *Give yourself permission to claim your courage.* Inertia is probably the first and most critical obstacle that holds us back on the job—the obstacle that prevents us from initiating everyday courage and moving forward. In inertia, life becomes unfulfilling and insipid. The discipline required to overcome this insidious obstacle requires you to "give yourself permission to claim your courage."

> *Confront uncomfortable truths head-on.* Only by learning to express ourselves from our own courageous identities can we truly begin to confront uncomfortable truths to overcome ambiguity, especially about ourselves.

> *Reveal vulnerability.* Revealing vulnerability exposes a person's true nature and undermines the ego tendency to get stuck in self-serving illusions.

> *Instill self-discipline.* The tendency to fall into the "average" mindset keeps us stuck in apathy versus instilling self-discipline.

> *Establish higher standards.* Failing to challenge ourselves to meet high standards keeps us trapped in a place of unrealized potential.

> *Motivate yourself from within.* Reflection is required to examine what truly troubles the spirit witnessed as sleepless nights or feeling disengaged at work.

> *Manifest your vision.* To allow your true self to manifest your best possible work situation requires your mind to be still and present (i.e., instead of replaying past moments or projecting future events).

> *Showcase your talents.* Do your talents energize others? How often do you stand animated and alone to showcase your talents? Are you comfortable in this potential awkwardness?

> *You must face obstacles head-on with all the facts in hand to make the best choices for the organization.*

Tackle the tough project. Are you a happy conduit enhancing the flow of success in your company, or has intimidation robbed you of a sense of purpose? Fear of failure is rapid in organizations and most people; yet, courageous leaders are willing to take on the tough project—the project no one wants such as making cold calls to start their business.

Hold yourself 100% accountable. Uncertainty may seem unavoidable in our age of information overload, bombarded as we are with contradictory "facts" from every quarter making it harder and harder to distinguish truth from falsehood.

By focusing your attention inward and following your heart, you strengthen your faith in your true, courageous self and step up, holding yourself 100% accountable.

Work without regrets. Recognizing your past regrets, you notice how fear kept you in prison until finally you learn to work without regrets. In this courage action you stop blaming (yourself and others).

Remove yourself from bad situations. Do you have a childhood "survival story" that you hold onto for dear life? Such stories are ego-created scripts that block your path to growth, but they can be overcome by adopting a personal meditative practice, which helps to uncover motivations obscured by the controlling tendencies of ego.[36]

In the end whether courage is spontaneous or learned, it is necessary when attempting to inspire others. Holding back or timidity will not generate inspiration. An inspirational leader must be intrepid but realistic in his/her assessment of situations and inspire through proper action, doing what is right.

INSPIRATION AND LEADERSHIP

Inspirational leadership in the LSI/GPS model leads to success by building upon the bulwark of credibility and competence. Those with high LSI inspire based on the value they place on the work and the people they work with. They also realize that inspiration is one of those elements of leadership that is best handled/produced with subtlety. That is while some actions/activities and utterances of a leader will clearly be design to inspire, true inspiration for both the leader and peers and followers comes from within by finding value and meaning in the work they do. The most successful leaders are those that inspire by being true to themselves and to the purpose of their organization.

Chapter 6

'Arriving at Your Destination'

Leader Vision

When planning a trip you generally start with your final destination in mind. So, for fun, let's imagine we are going on a trip to Disney World to ride the rides and see Mickey and Minnie. Or perhaps you'd prefer an imaginary trip to the Grand Canyon or Niagara Falls to see nature's awesome display, or even to Anchorage, Alaska, as a departure point for an Alaskan Cruise. Regardless of the destination, once you know where you want to go, and the address of the location you will be traveling to, the GPS can help you to arrive safely and timely.

If you don't have a destination in mind, or a plan for your vacation time, you might just spend it all at home. In order for a GPS to work effectively, you must have a vision about where you are heading. Once you have made that decision, the GPS will readily provide you with assistance about the best and quickest routes to get there.

The point is that the GPS is only a tool to take you to where *you* choose to go. You have to know where you want to go and program the GPS accordingly using the best detailed information you have or can obtain. Then trust the GPS to get you there. In like fashion, a leader must know where he/she wants an organization to go. A leader must have a vision of the organization's final destination and the path, including any side trips or stops along the way, to reach that destination. He/she must have or obtain the best detailed information that can be utilized to develop that vision and to carry it to fruition.

In the Leadership Intelligence (LSI) model, as in consideration of leadership in general, vision is a vital component of leadership success. Burt Nanus, a respected leader in vision research, shared:

A *vision* is a realistic, credible, attractive future for an organization. It is a carefully formulated statement of intentions that defines a destination or future state

65

of affairs that an individual or group finds particularly desirable. The right *vision* is an idea so powerful that it literally jump starts the future by calling forth the energies, talents, and resources to make things happen. A visionary leader is one who has the ability to formulate a compelling *vision* for the future of his or her organization, gain commitment to it, and translate that *vision* into reality by making the necessary organizational changes.[1]

From a somewhat different perspective, Collins and Porras say of vision, "A well-conceived vision consists of two major components: core ideology and envisioned future."[2] They describe these two components:

> Core ideology defines the enduring character of an organization—a consistent identity that transcends product or market life cycles, technological break-throughs, management fads, and individual leaders. In fact, the most lasting and significant contribution of those who build visionary companies is the core ideology.
>
> The second primary component of the vision framework is envisioned future. It consists of two parts: a 10-to-30-year audacious goals plus vivid descriptions of what it will be like to achieve the goal. We recognize that the phrase envisioned future is somewhat paradoxical. On the one hand, it conveys concrete-ness—something visible, vivid, and real. On the other hand, it involves a time yet unrealized—with its dreams, hopes, and aspirations.[3]

Bennis, in addressing twenty-first-century leadership said that "given the nature and constancy of change and the transnational challenges facing American business leadership, the key to making the right choices will come from understanding and embodying the leadership qualities necessary to suc-ceed in the volatile and mercurial global economy."[4] Of those qualities, he shared that "while leaders come in every size, shape, and disposition—short, tall, neat, sloppy, young, old, male, and female—there is at least one ingredi-ent that every leader I talked with shared: a concern with a guiding purpose, an overarching vision."[5]

Further, Bennis shared that "leaders have a clear idea of what they want to do—personally and professionally—and the strength to persist in the face of setbacks, even failures. They know where they are going, and why . . . I think of it this way: *Leaders manage the dream.*"[6] All leaders have the capacity to create a compelling vision, one that takes people to a new place, and then to translate that vision into reality.

Kouzes and Posner report based on their research:

> The number one requirement of a leader—honesty—was also the top-ranking attribute of a good colleague. But the second-highest requirement of a leader, that he or she be forward-looking, applied only to the leader role. Just 27% of

respondents selected it as something they want in a colleague, whereas 72% wanted it in a leader. (Among respondents holding more-senior roles in organizations, the percentage was even greater, at 88%.) No other quality showed such a dramatic difference between leader and colleague.[7]

In regard to leaders and vision, Kotter stated, "*Leaders* gather a broad range of data and look for patterns, relationships, and linkages that help explain things. *What's* more, the direction-setting aspect of leadership does not produce plans; it creates vision and strategies."[8] In further explanation, Kotter shared:

> Most discussions of vision have a tendency to degenerate into the mystical. The implication is that a vision is something mysterious that mere mortals, even talented ones, could never hope to have. But developing good business direction isn't magic. It is a tough, sometimes exhausting process of gathering and analyzing information. People who articulate such visions aren't magicians but broad-based strategic thinkers who are willing to take risks.
>
> Nor do visions and strategies have to be brilliantly innovative; in fact, some of the best are not. Effective business visions regularly have an almost mundane quality, usually consisting of ideas that are already well known. The particular combination or patterning of the ideas may be new, but sometimes even that is not the case.[9]

Similarly, in outlining the critical steps to successfully leading change, Kotter shared that one of the primary steps is "Creating a vision to help direct the change effort. Developing strategies for achieving that vision."[10]

In discussion of organizational success and the importance of promoting employee engagement, Goleman said, "If a leader is to articulate such shared values effectively, he or she must first look within to find a genuinely heartfelt guiding vision."[11] He held as well that, ". . . truly great, leaders need to expand their focus to a farther horizon line, even beyond decades, while taking their systems understanding to a much finer focus. And their leadership needs to reshape systems themselves."[12]

Stephen Covey listed vision as the first of four attributes of great leaders. Of vision, he said:

> *Vision.* Seeing a future state with the mind's eye is vision. It's applied imagination. All things are created twice: first, a mental creation; second, a physical creation. Vision starts the process of reinvention. It represents desire, dreams, hopes, goals, and plans. These dreams are not just fantasies—they are reality without physicality, like a construction blueprint. Most of us don't envision or realize our potential, even though we all have the power, energy, and capacity to reinvent our lives. Memory is past. It is finite. Vision is future. If is infinite.

The most important vision is having a sense of self, a sense of your own destiny, mission, role, purpose and meaning. When testing your own personal vision, first ask: Does the vision tap into my voice, energy, and talent? Does it give me a sense of "calling," a cause worthy of my commitment? Acquiring such meaning requires profound personal reflection to transcend our autobiography, rise above our memory, and create a magnanimity of spirit toward others. We need to consider not only the vision of what's possible "out there" but also the vision of what we see in other people, their unseen potential. Vision is about more than just getting things done; it is about discovering and expanding our view of others, affirming them, believing in them, and helping them discover their voice and realize their potential. Seeing people through the lens of their potential and their best actions, rather than through the lens of their current behavior or weaknesses, generates positive energy.[13]

Engaging others in the development and realization of the guiding vision for an organization is as important as the organizational vision of the leader. Organizations succeed not only on the work of the leader but more so on the work of the organizational members. Kouzes and Posner set forth the following steps to create a shared vision:

As counterintuitive as it might seem, then, the best way to lead people into the future is to connect with them deeply in the present. The only visions that take hold are shared visions—and you will create them only when you listen very, very closely to others, appreciate their hopes, and attend to their needs. The best leaders are able to bring their people into the future because they engage in the oldest form of research: They observe the human condition.[14]

Expanding on the requirements to create a shared vision, Kouzes and Posner state:

So how do new leaders develop this forward-looking capacity? First, of course, they must resolve to carve out time from urgent but endless operational matters. But even more important, as leaders spend more time looking ahead, they must not put too much stock in their own prescience. This point needs to be underscored because, somehow, through all the talk over the years about the importance of vision, many leaders have reached the unfortunate conclusion that they as individuals must be visionaries. With leadership development experts urging them along, they've taken to posing as emissaries from the future, delivering the news of how their markets and organizations will be transformed.

Bad idea! This is not what constituents want. Yes, leaders must ask, "What's new? What's next? What's better?"—but they can't present answers that are only theirs. Constituents want visions of the future that reflect their own aspirations. They want to hear how their dreams will come true and their hopes will be fulfilled. We draw this conclusion from our most recent analysis of nearly one million responses to our leadership assessment, "The Leadership Practices Inventory." The data tell us that what leaders struggle with most is communicating an image of the future that draws others in—that speaks to what others see and feel.[15]

Nanus said of gaining commitment of organizational members, "The key to gaining widespread commitment to a new vision, therefore, is to present the vision in such a way that people will want to participate and will freely choose to do so."[16] While the above examples spring from the business world, the same emphasis of vision is seen in the public sector. From a meta-analysis spanning the years 1995–2012, Murphy and Torre conclude that "Vision is a hallmark variable in the school improvement algorithm. Second, leadership is the keystone element in developing, implementing, and shepherding the school's vision."[17]

Méndez-Morse, writing for the Southwest Educational Development Laboratory, stated:

Visionary educational leaders have a clear picture of what they want to accomplish. The vision of their school or district provides purpose, meaning, and significance to the work of the school and enables them to motivate and empower the staff to contribute to the realization of the vision . . . In addition to providing a picture of the future, a vision inspires people to work to make it come true. It motivates people to join the campaign to realize the desired vision.[18]

She goes onto to share four steps to developing a shared vision.[19] According to Méndez-Morse, these four steps facilitate a collaborative development of a shared vision and written vision statement. These steps are as follows:

1. *Know your organization*—Clarify the nature and purpose
2. *Involve critical individuals*—Include those affected
3. *Explore the possibilities*—Consider possible futures
4. *Put it in writing*—Vision is committed to paper[20]

Vision as defined in the LSI model is the end result of a process whereby a leader develops objectives or goals and sets a direction for an organization based on the shared input of all stakeholders. Defining vision is simple. Creating a shared vision and, more significantly, effectively communicating that shared vision and transforming it into action is the challenge. The components discussed in the remainder of this chapter, commitment, sense of direction, professionalism, decisiveness, work ethic, and concern for the future form the basis of leadership vision in the LSI model.

COMMITMENT

Commitment is the cornerstone on which vision is built. It is the desire and dedication by the leader to pursue a given objective or set of objectives or goals for an organization. Crossan et al. put forth:

> In assessing leaders at any level in an organization, we must always ask three questions:
>
> 1. Do they have the *competencies* to be a leader? Do they have the knowledge, the understanding of key concepts, facts, and relationships that they need to do the job effectively?
> 2. Do they have the *commitment* to be a leader? Yes, they aspire to be a leader, but are they prepared to do the hard work of leadership, engage with others in fulfilling the organizational mission, achieve the vision and deliver on the goals?
> 3. Do they have the *character* to be a good leader and strive to be an even better one? Do they have the values, traits and virtues that others—shareholders, employees, customers, suppliers, regulators and the broader society within which they operate—will use to determine if they are good leaders?[21]

As Crossan et al.'s second question suggests, commitment calls for the leader to provide both the initial impetus to develop and layout a vision and a direction for an organization and the commitment to put forth the effort on a continuing basis to stay the course in the face of obstacles to see that vision to fruition. That is, it is expected that the leader will display a willingness to be flexible or change as circumstances change or exigencies arise that were heretofore unforeseen. Leadership commitment takes on many forms.

Commitment can be evidenced in the time a leader invests in his/her work for the organization: devoting more than the required forty hours at work; devoting time after normal work hours; exhibiting low or no absenteeism; making maximum use of his/her available time; and, valuing the time of others through appropriate scheduling. Commitment by the leader is exhibited through the organizational work that he/she accomplishes either individually or as a part of an organizational team. Visibility, availability, and openness to discussion and input are also clear markers of leadership commitment.

A leader who is committed cares about the organization as an entity but also cares about the individuals that make up the organization, and is concerned about the relationship of the organization and its membership to the people and other organizations external to his/her organization. A committed leader works diligently to balance the needs of the organization with his/her own professional needs, the needs of the members of the organization, and the audience/wider world external to the organization. Nanus said the following about what leaders must do to establish his/her commitment:

Leaders live the vision by making all their actions and behaviors consistent with it and by creating a sense of urgency and passion for its attainment. You can do this in many ways, among them the following:

How you make and honor commitments.
What you say in formal and especially informal settings.
What you express interests in and what questions you ask.
Where you choose to go and with whom you spend your time.
When you choose to act and how you make your actions known.
How you organize your staff and your physical surroundings.[22]

Sarros et al. equate commitment with loyalty and share that "leaders who demonstrate organisational loyalty show a deep commitment to building organisational sustainability. Such leaders have been described as having the resolve to do whatever it takes to make a company great irrespective how hard the decisions or how difficult the task."[23]

Leaders must not only show commitment themselves but strive to gain commitment to the shared vision from organizational members. Steyrer et al. in a study of "the effect of executive leadership behaviors on the organizational commitment (OC)" found that "our results also support the claim that OC has beneficial effects for company performance." What is more, they found that "leadership behavior which is strong on dimensions that are perceived as prototypical of an ideal leader has positive effects."[24]

The 'prototypical' leadership behaviors Steyrer references are those identified in the Globe Study.[25] The Globe Study lists vision as one of the "most universally desirable" leader characteristics.[26] To be truly visionary for an organization a leader must be committed to that organization.

Consider FDR and his vision and commitment to the presidency.[27] After having led the United States out of the Great Depression and through a time of extreme crisis, he re-committed his energy and enthusiasm to serving the country not one more term, but three. The only president elected to office four consecutive terms, Roosevelt's vision, optimism, and commitment in light of his formidable health issues were quite amazing.

Perhaps his ability to communicate effectively with America via his fireside chats was a part of his overall success. Hamm posits that communication is the key-gaining commitment. He says:

I've come to the conclusion that the real job of leadership is to inspire the organization to take responsibility for creating a better future. I believe effective communication is a leader's single most critical management tool for making this happen. When leaders take the time to explain what they mean, both explicitly (by carefully defining their visions, intentions, and directions) and implicitly (through their behavior), they assert much-needed influence over the vague but powerful notions that otherwise run away with employees' imaginations.

By clarifying amorphous terms and commanding and managing the corporate vocabulary, leaders effectively align precious employee energy and commitment within their organizations.[28]

Feiner, a former Pepsi Cola top executive, coined what he called the "Law of Personal Commitment."[29] It states that *"if a leader wants a subordinate to be committed to the success of the leader and the leader's organization, then the leader must be committed to the subordinate*—to his or her growth and development, and to what's important to him or her both inside and outside the office."

When a leader is committed to an organization and its vision and goals and is able to generate organizational commitment, the probability of the organizational success increases exponentially.

SENSE OF DIRECTION

To succeed a leader must have a clear sense of organizational direction. Initially that sense of direction is embodied in the shared organizational vision. That vision is typically developed when he/she joins the organization or, perhaps, receives an internal promotion and assumes a leadership role within the organization. Just as the leader uses a group process to develop a shared vision, he/she must engage organizational members to devise and carry out a plan to move the organization from where it is toward the vision-based destination. The plan or plans developed will vary tremendously based on the type of enterprise.

But regardless of the enterprise, there are commonalities in leadership behaviors that indicate that he/she has a sense of direction for the organization. The first step most often taken is to develop a strategic plan, followed by development and implementation of action plans. Once the actions plans are operational, monitoring begins. Final steps are assessment of progress/level of success and realignment as needed. Yukl and Lepsinger state that "a brilliant strategy is of little value unless it can be implemented effectively.[30]

The process of translating strategy into successful business results and maintaining efficient, reliable operations is commonly called *execution*, and it is one of the essential challenges for leaders in today's business environment, where rapid and complex change is the norm." Based on a survey of business leaders they propose four steps (leadership behaviors) to promote 'execution' of strategy:

- *Operational planning*
- *Clarifying roles and objectives*

- *Monitoring operations and performance*
- *Solving operational problems*

Operational planning. This leadership behavior involves determining short-term objectives and action steps for achieving them; determining how to use personnel, equipment, facilities, and other resources efficiently to accomplish a project or initiative; and determining how to schedule and coordinate the activities of various individuals, teams, and work units.

Clarifying roles and objectives. This leadership behavior involves the communication of responsibilities, role expectations, and performance objectives to direct reports, peers, and outsiders who make an important contribution to work-unit performance.

Monitoring operations and performance. This leadership behavior involves gathering information about work activities, checking on the progress and quality of the work, and evaluating individual and unit performance.

Solving operational problems. This leadership behavior involves identifying work issues, analyzing them in a systematic but timely manner, and acting decisively to implement solutions.

Walinskas addressed the issue of creating a direction when he said, "As long as the management knows where we're going, we'll get there, right? No, wrong! Everyone needs to be singing from the same song sheet. How do you, as a leader, communicate the corporate vision so that people willingly follow and perform at their highest possible levels? Here are some tips:

- *Reason.* People aren't really lemmings. The main corporate *vision* has to be communicated along with a why the change must take place.
- *Repetition.* Repetition is the father of learning.
- *Action orientation.* If the *vision* statement itself has action verbs instead of the verb "to be" in it, it motivates people to put it into practice.
- *Multi-sensory education.* Communicating an organizational *vision* is nothing more than educating. People learn it and how adhering to it affects their lives. But people learn in different ways
- *Stimulate emotions.* People act based on emotion. Later, if necessary, they justify their actions with facts. Every trained salesperson knows this. And a leader trying to communicate the corporate *vision* is simply a salesperson.
- *Empower them.* People like to feel important."[31]

Jensen offers similar reasoning, but applied to mid-level managers of whom he says, "Leadership, particularly midlevel leadership, is the foundation of success." He too provides a process for implementing vision, providing a sense of direction. He shares the following:

- *Supporting goals and objectives: fixing responsibility.* The organizational philosophy is the foundation of the strategic plan, but strategic goals with supporting objectives must be developed. Goals describe a future condition that the organization needs to attain to achieve its vision. Objectives are statements of what must be done to achieve a goal.
- *Detailed action planning: where the rubber meets the road.* Each objective should have an action plan. An action plan describes the specific tasks that are necessary to achieve the supported objective.
- *Measurements: understanding progress.* Measuring specific tasks is necessary to understand progress against expected results.
- *Environmental scanning: assessing opportunities and threats.* A strategic plan is a living document. Changes and updates to the plan are driven by the strategic environment, those factors outside the organization that are potential opportunities or threats.
- *Leadership emphasis: a strategic-planning imperative.* Employees pay attention to what is important to the boss. For the strategic plan to be effectively executed, it must be a top priority of leadership at all levels.[32]

Dewan and Mayatt, in discussion of leadership in the political arena but applicable in any field, share that "A leader's influence increases with her judgment (her sense of direction) and her ability to convey ideas (her clarity of communication)."[33] Nanus said, "Vision is little more than an empty dream until it is widely shared and accepted. Only then does it acquire the force necessary to change an organization and move it in the intended direction."[34] He sees communication, networking, and "living the dream" as the primary means a leader should use to create acceptance and thereby move the organization toward achievement of the vision.

As the organization moves toward achieving its vision that vision must be renewed over time. As Nanus stated, "There is no regular schedule for revising a vision."[35] At some point, however, signals from monitoring or tracking activities may suggest the need for altering or perhaps even replacing the vision. The leader must be responsible for establishing the time frame and conditions which will prompt reappraisal, renewal, and reestablishment of the organizational vision and concomitant goals, objectives, and actions. The cyclical process of renewal provides the organization with a continuing sense of direction and allows the organization to be continuously on the cutting edge in its area.

A great example of a visionary with a sense of direction was David Packard, co-founder, CEO, and president of Hewlett-Packard, one of the largest electronic testing and measurement device companies of its time.[36] But before Packard rose to this sort of distinction, he was a very self-confident man who knew where he was headed. It is said of Packard that in the late 50s he was in a meeting with a cast of businessmen trying to sort out how to make their companies more profitable.

Packard quickly asserted his belief that the organization was much more than the bottom line. He felt a true need to support his employees first. Packard stated that he was surprised that no one in the meeting stepped up to agree with him. This experience made him feel like an outsider while making him realize that others did not feel he had the mentality to be a CEO.

PROFESSIONALISM

Professionalism provides the lens through which leaders can engage in reflective self-criticism to become better leaders. The same lens allows followers to judge the work-related utterances and actions of the leader. For many leaders, their concept of professionalism is based on a code of conduct, professional standards, or code of ethics for their field. Many large organizations memorialize these in official documents. For example, Google's code of conduct (which is seventeen pages in length) reads in part:[37]

"Don't be evil." Googler's generally apply those words to how we serve our users. But "Don't be evil" is much more than that. Yes, it's about providing our users unbiased access to information, focusing on their needs and giving them the best products and services that we can. But it's also about doing the right thing more generally—following the law, acting honorably and treating each other with respect (emphasis added).

The Google Code of Conduct is one of the ways we put "Don't be evil" into practice. It's built around the recognition that everything we do in connection with our work at Google will be, and should be, measured against the highest possible standards of ethical business conduct (emphasis added). We set the bar that high for practical as well as aspirational reasons: Our commitment to the highest standards helps us hire great people, build great products, and attract loyal users. Trust and mutual respect among employees and users are the foundation of our success, and they are something we need to earn every day.

So please do read the Code, and follow both its spirit and letter, always bearing in mind that each of us has a personal responsibility to incorporate, and to encourage other Googler's to incorporate, the principles of the Code into our work.

Who Must Follow Our Code?

We expect all of our employees and Board members to know and follow the Code. Failure to do so can result in disciplinary action, including termination of employment. Moreover, while the Code is specifically written for Google employees and Board members, we expect Google contractors, consultants and others who may be temporarily assigned to perform work or services for Google to follow the Code in connection with their work for us. Failure of a Google contractor, consultant or other covered service provider to follow the Code can result in termination of their relationship with Google (emphasis added).

Ford Corporation provides another example (by comparison the Ford handbook is sixty pages in length):

> Ford Motor Company is committed to conducting business fairly and honestly. This commitment to integrity requires each of us to act ethically. Each of us is expected to act, at all times and in all circumstances, with the highest sense of integrity on behalf of the Company. We are expected to act in a manner that protects and enhances the Company's corporate reputation
>
> Remember, anyone who violates the law or a Company Policy may be subject to disciplinary action, up to and including termination or release (emphasis added).[38]

J. P. Morgan Chase and Co. shares the following about their code of ethics (actual document is sixty pages):

Code of Ethics for Finance Professionals

This Code of Ethics for Finance Professionals applies to the Chief Executive Officer, President, Chief Financial Officer, and Chief Accounting Officer of JPMorgan Chase & Co. (the "firm") and to all other professionals of the firm worldwide serving in a finance, accounting, corporate treasury, tax or investor relations role.

The purpose of this Code of Ethics for Finance Professionals is to promote honest and ethical conduct and compliance with the law, particularly as related to the maintenance of the firm's financial books and records and the preparation of its financial statements. The obligations of this Code of Ethics for Finance Professionals supplement, but do not replace, the firm's Code of Conduct. As a finance professional of the firm, you are expected to:

- Engage in and promote ethical conduct, including the ethical handling of actual or apparent conflicts of interest between personal and professional relationships, and to disclose to the Office of the Secretary any material transaction or relationship that reasonably could be expected to give rise to such a conflict.
- Carry out your responsibilities honestly, in good faith and with integrity, due care and diligence, exercising at all times the best independent judgment.
- Assist in the production of full, fair, accurate, timely and understandable disclosure in reports and documents that the firm and its subsidiaries file with, or submit to, the Securities and Exchange Commission and other regulators and in other public communications made by the firm.
- Comply with applicable government laws, rules and regulations of federal, state and local governments and other appropriate regulatory agencies.
- Promptly report (anonymously, if you wish to do so) to the Audit Committee of the Board of Directors any violation of this Code of Ethics or any other matters that would compromise the integrity of the firm's financial

statements. You may contact the Audit Committee by mail, by phone, or by e-mail; contact information is set forth below.

- Never to take, directly or indirectly, any action to coerce, manipulate, mislead or fraudulently influence the firm's independent auditors in the performance of their audit or review of the firm's financial statements.

Compliance with this Code of Ethics for Finance Professionals is a term and condition of your employment. The firm will take all necessary actions to enforce this Code, up to and including immediate dismissal (emphasis added). Violations of this Code of Ethics for Finance Professionals may also constitute violations of law, which may expose both you and the firm to criminal or civil penalties and add the link in the notes.[39]

The level of concern for professionalism is evidenced further by the adoption (starting with the graduating class of 2009) by the Harvard School of Business MBA Oath. Max Anderson, one of the class members for the class that initiated the oath, shared about creating the oath:

I am part of a team of 25 graduating Harvard MBAs who created the MBA Oath, pledging to lead professional careers marked with integrity and ethics. My classmates and I are aware of the low opinion many people have of MBAs, especially in the wake of the financial crisis. We don't want to be known as the least respected profession in America (though some polls say MBAs hold that distinction). We want to be known as professionals, who look after the best interests of their clients, customers, employees and shareholders.[40]

That oath reads:

As a manager, my purpose is to serve the greater good by bringing together people and resources to create value that no single individual can build alone. Therefore, I will seek a course that enhances the value my enterprise can create for society over the long term. I recognize that my decisions can have far-reaching consequences that affect the well-being of individuals inside and outside my enterprise, today and in the future. As I reconcile the interests of different constituencies, I will face difficult choices.

Therefore, I promise:

1. I will act with utmost integrity and pursue my work in an ethical manner.
2. I will safeguard the interests of my shareholders, co-workers, customers and the society in which we operate.
3. I will manage my enterprise in good faith, guarding against decisions and behavior that advance my own narrow ambitions but harm the enterprise and the societies it serves.
4. I will understand and uphold, both in letter and in spirit, the laws and contracts governing my own conduct and that of my enterprise.

5. I will take responsibility for my actions, and will represent the performance and risks of my enterprise accurately and honestly.
6. I will develop both myself and other managers under my supervision so that the profession continues to grow and contribute to the well-being of society.
7. I will strive to create sustainable economic, social, and environmental prosperity worldwide.
8. I will be accountable to my peers and they will be accountable to me for living by this oath.

This oath I make freely, and upon my honor.

Private sector professionals such as doctors, lawyers, and engineers operate under similar codes of conduct/ethics. The American Medical Association provides:

An important division of the AMA, the Ethics Group works to improve patient care and the health of the public by examining and promoting physician professionalism. If you're looking for guidance or insight to ethical issues in medicine today, the AMA Ethics Group offers relevant resources to help you such as the Code of Medical Ethics.

The AMA Ethics Group is responsible for helping establish ethical policies, developing educational programs and pursuing scholarly research of ethical issues in medicine that practicing physicians are likely to encounter in their training and daily practice.[41]

For attorneys, the wording of the codes of professionalism vary from state to state and/or federal court jurisdictions. The American Bar Association maintains a file of these "Professionalism Codes."[42] The sample below is from the Arizona Bar Association:

A Lawyer's Creed of Professionalism of the State Bar of Arizona

Preamble

As a lawyer I must strive to make our system of justice work fairly and efficiently. In order to carry out that responsibility, I will comply with the letter and spirit of the disciplinary standards applicable to all lawyers and I will conduct myself in accordance with the following Creed of Professionalism when dealing with my client, opposing parties, their counsel, tribunals and the general public.

Engineers subscribe to the code of conduct of the National Society of Professional Engineers (NSPE) Code of Ethics for Engineers.[43] That code reads in part:

Engineering is an important and learned profession. As members of this profession, engineers are expected to exhibit the highest standards of honesty and integrity. Engineering has a direct and vital impact on the quality of life for all people. Accordingly, the services provided by engineers require honesty, impartiality, fairness, and equity, and must be dedicated to the protection of the public health, safety, and welfare. Engineers must perform under a standard of professional behavior that requires adherence to the highest principles of ethical conduct.

Public sector leaders and organizational members are often subject to similar professional conduct expectations. For example, educational leaders are trained in accordance with the standards set forth in the Professional Standards for Educational Leaders (formerly the Interstate Leaders Licensure Consortium—ISLLC) developed by the National Policy Board for Educational Administration. The Professional Standards for Educational Leaders standards most closely related to professionalism reads:

Standard 2: Ethics and Professional Norms

Effective educational leaders act ethically and according to professional norms to promote *each* student's academic success and well-being.

Effective leaders:

a) Act ethically and professionally in personal conduct, relationships with others, decision making, stewardship of the school's resources, and all aspects of school leadership.
b) Act according to and promote the professional norms of integrity, fairness, transparency, trust, collaboration, perseverance, learning, and continuous improvement.
c) Place children at the center of education and accept responsibility for each student's academic success and well-being.
d) Safeguard and promote the values of democracy, individual freedom and responsibility, equity, social justice, community, and diversity.
e) Lead with interpersonal and communication skill, social-emotional insight, and understanding of all students' and staff members' backgrounds and cultures.
f) Provide moral direction for the school and promote ethical and professional behavior among faculty and staff.[44]

These same standards are often carried over into school leader evaluation instruments developed by state or local governing authorities. The Oregon State Department of Education states, for example:

Oregon Educational Leadership/Administrator Standards

These standards guide administrative preparation, licensure and job performance. Oregon's educational leadership/administrator standards align with the

Interstate School Leaders Licensure Consortium (ISLLC) and the Educational Leadership Constituents Council (ELCC) 2009 standards for Educational Leadership.

Performance Expectations and Indicators for Education Leaders Education Leadership (SCEL)

The performance expectations and indicators represent consensus among state education agency policy leaders about the most important actions required of K–12 education leaders to improve teaching and learning.[45]

Reading the corporate code examples of organizations lends itself to understanding the importance of the documents as each document states that failure to abide by the code espoused is grounds for termination. Whether explicitly included in a document or not as the second set of examples illustrates, it is generally clearly understood that failure to act in accordance with codes of conduct/ethics or professional standards may result in loss of employment.

The standards for the professions listed, as well as example standards listed for public sector leaders, while they do not necessarily state explicitly that termination will result from a breach of the code or standard, it is widely accepted that failure to follow the prescribed code or abide by the standards will result in either sanctions (license suspension) and/or termination from employment or both. Unfortunately, we have far too often seen leaders depart from the behavior provided by the codes/standards with tragic personal and professional results as well as inestimable damage to organizational members.

Acting professionally adds to the ability of a leader to engage in pursuit of organizational vision and to engage others in that pursuit. Acting professionally also allows a leader to reflect on his/her work in comparison to those standards and insure that his/her behavior aligns with the standards. Organizational members likewise know that the leader is bound by these standards and can easily form an opinion as to the professional behavior of the leader. For those leaders who act professionally the reward is full engagement by the organization's members. For those who do not act professionally the opposite is true, they will struggle to elicit positive engagement.

DECISIVE

Prime Minister Margaret Thatcher knew exactly what it was in which she believed. Not only did she have strong beliefs, but she was decisive in her manner regarding those beliefs. Not long after taking office, Thatcher vehemently shared that "we should not expect the state to appear in the guise of an extravagant good fairy at every christening, a loquacious companion at every stage of life's journey, and the unknown mourner at every funeral."[46] And, Thatcher believed this in spite of the fact that she did not have large support in her thinking. However, she was quick to learn how to lead those who saw things differently.

Decisiveness is the mechanism by which a leader guides the organization in the direction set forth by the shared vision for the organization. He/she makes decisions that align with that vision and that promote or enhance organizational members' ability to carry out needed tasks to fulfill that vision. Those decisions may have minimal observable affect or they may change the course of the organization in radical ways shattering long held beliefs or practices. Regardless of the importance of the decision, it is essential to leader and organizational success that appropriate and timely decisions be made.

As Tasler said, "Strategic decisiveness is one of the most vital success attributes for leaders in every position and every industry."[47] And further, he shared that "it is not surprising that picking one strategic direction and then decisively pursuing that direction are hallmarks of good leadership."[48] In the *Handbook of Leadership Theory and Practice*, Useem shares that "Leadership requires a strategic vision and a sense of mission. It requires an ability to excite and to execute. It requires unflinching determination, impeccable character, and a commitment to common cause over private gain. But it also requires an exceptional capacity to make good and timely decisions."[49]

Given the importance of decisiveness, it is vital as well to understand that decisions must have an ethical basis to be accepted. To that end, Howard and Korver, suggest that "We must *master ethical distinctions* to enable clear ethical thinking. We must *commit in advance to ethical principles*. And we must *exercise disciplined decision-making skills* to choose wisely."[50]

Of choosing wisely Howard and Korver say, "By pinpointing the principles we hold dear, consciously or unconsciously drawn from religion, upbringing, and culture, we prepare thoroughly. Only then, when the principles we articulate resonate with our inner voice, can we say we are ready to mindfully follow standards that underpin skillful ethical decision making."[51]

It is equally important that a leader conveys the significance of sound decision making to all organizational members and establishes a consistent process for making decisions. Returning once more to the butterfly effect, recall that even a very small decision made at the base level of an organization can have unforeseen but substantial affect. Peter Drucker, in his seminal work on decision-making, said:

> Effective executives know when a decision has to be based on principle and when it should be made pragmatically, on the merits of the case. They know the trickiest decision is that between the right and the wrong compromise, and they

have learned to tell one from the other. They know that the most time-consuming step in the process is not making the decision but putting it into effect. Unless a decision has degenerated into work, it is not a decision; it is at best a good intention. This means that, while the effective decision itself is based on the highest level of conceptual understanding, the action commitment should be as close as possible to the capacities of the people who have to carry it out. Above all, effective executives know that decision making has its own systematic process and its own clearly defined elements.[52]

And, he set forth a decision-making process of 'Sequential Steps':[53]

1. *Classifying the problem.* Is it generic? Is it exceptional and unique? Or is it the first manifestation of a new genus for which a rule has yet to be developed?
2. *Defining the problem.* What are we dealing with?
3. *Specifying the answer to the problem.* What are the "boundary conditions"?
4. *Deciding what is "right," rather than what is acceptable, in order to meet the boundary conditions . . .* What will fully satisfy the specifications *before* attention is given to the compromises, adaptations, and concessions needed to make the decision acceptable?
5. *Building into the decision the action to carry it out.* What does the action commitment have to be? Who has to know about it?
6. *Testing the validity and effectiveness of the decision against the actual course of events.* How is the decision being carried out? Are the assumptions on which it is based appropriate or obsolete?

The elements do not by themselves 'make' the decisions. Indeed, every decision is a risk-taking judgment. But unless these elements are the stepping stones of the decision process, the executive will not arrive at a right, and certainly not at an effective, decision.

Neal and Spetzler in more recent work suggest the use of the Decision Quality (DQ) Model. They relate that "DQ (is) a process that defines a high-quality decision as the course of action that will capture the most value or get the most of what you are seeking, given the uncertainties and complexities of the real world."[54] The DQ process contains the following steps:

• An appropriate frame, including a clear understanding of the problem and what needs to be achieved.
• Creative, doable alternatives from which to choose the one likely to achieve the most of what you want.
• Meaningful information that is reliable, unbiased, and reflects all relevant uncertainties and intangibles.
• Clarity about desired outcomes, including acceptable tradeoffs.

- Solid reasoning and sound logic that includes considerations of uncertainty and insight at the appropriate level of complexity.
- Commitment to action by all stakeholders necessary to achieve effective action.

Decisiveness allows a leader to show commitment and a sense of direction. He/she focuses organizational efforts by the decisions he/she makes. That is, by guiding/influencing decisions related to the people, materials, and processes that are necessary underpinnings of the organizational vision the leader can establish and reinforce the strategic plan for achieving the vision. As Nanus notes, "You can shape the social context in ways to suit your vision, especially through the decisions you make and commitments about the following:

- Who you choose to assign to groups and tasks
- The amount and types of resources and support services you make available to work groups
- The design of incentive systems
- The way jobs are structured and allocated among work groups
- Your choice of people to head the teams
- The goals and expectations you associate with each organizational unit."[55]

Put simply, effective leaders use the decision-making process in combination with the vision of the organization as a driving force in the organization. They make timely and focused decisions and establish processes that allow others within the organization to engage in structured but flexible decision making. When decisions are vision focused at all levels of leadership and among the rank and file, the prospect of success is greatly enhanced.

WORK ETHIC

One example of having a work ethic imprinted early can be found in the Rev. Billy Graham. As a boy, the family alarm chimed at 2:30 a.m. for the farm to be worked. Billy's responsibility was to tend the cows. The twenty dairy cows had to be milked every morning and afternoon as well as having their hay troughs refilled and the manure being cleaned out of the barn twice daily.[56]

Today, we are aware of many stories of leaders who make a habit of being the first to arrive at work and the last to leave. Such devotion may be called for by some professions and reflects a strong work ethic. Or perhaps it reflects a need to develop a competitive advantage or even simply to provide the time for sustained reflection. But, whether being the first into and last out the office is needed or desirable, it does tend to set a tone for the organization.

If the leader is willing to commit his/her time and effort the work must have value. It is this work value that most profoundly impacts the leader's vision in relation to work. As Woodward shared, "Values control the choice of organizational goals thereby serving as standards through which decisions are assessed."[57] And further that "work values impact employees' performance decisions by providing criteria for choosing a particular behaviour or action over an alternative."[58] And finally, speaking to the leader's view of work value:

> With respect to leaders' perspective, values might not essentially affect the choice of a purpose, but they act as means through which purpose can be monitored. They can guide leaders by impacting ideas about potential directions and help them to understand, as well as decide, what they will be comfortable with in relation to organizational strategy, functioning and direction.[59]

As with other aspects of leadership, work ethic is more than what the leader does. He/she is also modeling, leading by example, and inspiring others to develop and exhibit a strong work ethic. Woodward states that "leadership, organizational and team performance is profoundly influenced by values."[60] That is, if the leader places value on a strong work ethic, it is likely that organizations members, if they respect and trust the leader, will value a strong work ethic as well.

As Church found in study of manager behavior and group work climate, "The more the leaders of this organization are seen as demonstrating an ethical concern for how business is done and the more they are trusted to 'do the right thing,' the more employees will feel that their work has significance and meaning and their talents are being utilized, and the more satisfied they will be overall."[61] Similarly Meriac et al. in a study of work ethic and task persistence found that "In general, these results indicate that work ethic, and in particular morality/ethics, is related to task motivation."[62]

Pat Summit was a leader with a great work ethic.[63] As a matter of fact, the Lady Vols basketball coach, the winningest coach in NCAA basketball history, never missed a day of school from kindergarten through high school. Having a strong work ethic was just a part of "Trish's" life. Bent on signing up a potential recruit, she flew to Pennsylvania extremely close to the due date of her first child. On the plane on the trip home, her water broke. Talk about work ethic. Summit urged the pilots not to stop prematurely so that her son would be born in Tennessee.

Work ethic promotes leader vision by setting the bar of performance for both the leader and organizational members. While not all members will place the same value on work ethic as the leader, without a visionary emphasis of the importance of the work to be done and the potential for success through hard work, the results will fall short of expectations.

CONCERN FOR THE FUTURE

Leaders who show concern for the future often include in their vision organizational goals and objectives that will almost surely postdate their tenure. The vision may be for better facilities, more personnel, expansion of services or products, or greater commitment to research and development with an eye toward innovation. Concerned leaders hope to build upon current organizational success and forward the sustainability of organizational success.

Most leaders have an innate desire to leave an organization in better shape than when they joined it, whether that is through building success, sustaining success, or projecting success into the future through innovation in their field. Of innovative leadership and the future, Doss says:

> The future is where innovation always lives, and sometimes that future is a long way off, uncertain, and really hard to forecast. Those who wish to be true leaders of innovation must be able to meet urgent, near-term demands, and at the same time serve as role models for the future . . . without worrying too much about the specifics of that future. The seeds of culture and risk and trust that you sow as an innovation leader of the *now* will only manifest themselves at some future, unpredictable time and place. Be *in* the present; be *about* the future. You will have lots of company worrying about that next board meeting, or that next quarterly report; but *as a leader of innovation you may find your concern for the future to be a lonely spot. Stay there.*[64]

Doss's point is well taken. The day-to-day grind tends to wear down even the most dedicated and concerned leader as the burden of leadership is substantial. Rarely does a leader on his first day with an organization start thinking about where his/her organization will be in thirty years; and, on a more personal level, it is equally rare for a leader to start thinking about his/her retirement on his/her first day in a new organization. In both instances, the tasks at hand overshadow considerations of the distant future.

However, that is not to say that concern for the future is only about the distant future with no consideration for the near or short term (three to five years) or even the slightly more distant future (six to ten years) or more (greater than ten years). A concerned leader is concerned about all of the forgoing time frames.

Golda Meir was thus concerned for her country. Her whole life reflected her desire to see the success of her people and her country. She became prime minister of Israel at the age of seventy, a time when most people are considering, if not already, retired. Meir hated war and even the loss of lives of those who opposed Israel. A famous Meir quote was "when peace comes we will perhaps in time be able to forgive the Arabs for killing our sons, but it will be harder for us to forgive them for having forced us to kill their sons."[65] She was a great woman of peace and one who was desperately concerned for the future of Israel.

Peter Drucker said regarding the ability to look ahead, "In human affairs— political, social, economic, or business—it is pointless to try to predict the future, let alone attempt to look ahead 75 years. But it is possible—and fruitful—to identify major events that have already happened, irrevocably, and that will have predictable effects in the next decade or two."[66] It is possible, in other words, to identify and prepare for the future *that has already happened*. When Drucker's concept is applied to the continuous renewal of organizational vision; the future blends with the present to produce constant forward movement.

But as Bennis noted, as leaders pass through stages in their careers they come to a point where consideration of the future, both theirs and the organizations, becomes a central focus. Bennis, in his article, *The Seven Ages of the Leader*, shared that this change in leader perspective comes about during the sixth career stage which he labeled, 'The Statesman, with Spectacles on Nose.' The leader in this stage is often 'hard at work preparing to pass on his or her wisdom in the interest of the organization.'[67]

Passing the baton involves the succession process. That is helping to determine who a successor will be or at least the characteristics, skills, and dispositions his/her successor should have. The degree of involvement will vary with the organization and the individual leader but for the leader it is an important consideration. Continued success reflects well on his/her legacy. Of course a concerned leader will have surrounded himself/herself with a cadre of leadership talent over the course of their career: this is unobtrusive in practice as it occurs in the natural course of personnel change with an organization, but it is vital to the success of the organization in the long term. As Conger shared:

> In our research into the factors that contribute to a leader's success or failure, we've found that certain companies do succeed in developing deep and enduring bench strength by approaching succession planning as more than the mechanical process of updating a list. Indeed, they've combined two practices—succession planning and leadership development--to create a long-term process for managing the talent roster across their organizations. In most companies, the two practices reside in separate functional silos, but they are natural allies because they share a vital and fundamental goal: getting the right skills in the right place.[68]

Succession planning though is not a universal practice (though it should be), as Bower noted:

> I WAS APPALLED TO LEARN RECENTLY that 60% of the respondents to a poll of 1,380 HR directors of large U.S. companies said their firms have no CEO succession plans in place. As this finding suggests, too many companies have over the past two decades ignored the hard work of building future leaders while senior executives have focused increasingly on meeting the next quarter's earnings target.[69]

Careers start and careers end but in most instances, especially for educators, the organization continues on. By articulating an organizational vision that addresses both short-term and long-range goals and renewing that vision periodically, a leader can impact an organization long after he/she has moved on into retirement or to another organization. Leaders who have genuine concern for the future plan for the future. Their well-honed leadership intelligence tells them it is the right thing to do, and their visionary nature provides the vehicle for that vision.

VISION AND LEADERSHIP

A leader without a vision for the organization will surely fail. Vision is truly that critical to overall success as a leader. The vision can be short term and renewed frequently or long term with strategic adjustments made at greater intervals, but it must exist. Change is the one constant in life that few, if any, would dispute. Leader vision addresses not only the current tasks but the future of the organization. It is the impetus that generates forward thinking and the ongoing incorporation of new discoveries and innovations. Vision opens the door for the credible, competent, inspirational leader to opportunities for success.

Chapter 7

'Route Guidance Suggested'

Leader Emotional Intelligence

With dynamic route guidance, as opposed to static route guidance, if traffic messages about delays, slow-moving traffic, congestion, or road closures are received, the GPS checks whether the affected area can be avoided and directs the driver on a newly computed alternative route. Dynamic route guidance provides the most favorable routes available, so that traffic flows and congestion situations will not occur so frequently.

The final destination can be reached with a minimum of delays, difficulty, and rerouting. For leaders, having a dynamic route guidance system is of utmost importance to success. It will not only provide a means for evaluating the potential for getting to the final destination, if/as issues arise, it will provide the best alternative route.

The Leadership Intelligence (LSI) model views emotional intelligence (EI) as the source of dynamic route guidance for leaders. EI helps a leader find the right path to follow while taking into account congestion (multiple recommendations for alternate solutions or different visions for the leader and organization), road closures (situations in which cooperation or input is needed but unavailable), and rerouting (the need to be flexible in meeting organizational needs and the needs of organizational members as well as consumers). EI enables a credible, competent leader who has the ability to inspire others to engage organizational members in developing and implementing a shared organizational vision.

The research and commentary regarding EI paints in broad strokes the importance of this concept. It is the basis for a great deal of the human interaction that occurs in an organization. Daniel Goleman, a widely recognized expert in EI, holds:

The most effective leaders are alike in one crucial way: they all have a high degree of what has come to be known as emotional intelligence.

It's not that IQ and technical skills are irrelevant. They do matter, but mainly as 'threshold capabilities;' that is, they are the entry-level requirements for executive positions. But my research, along with other recent studies, clearly shows that emotional intelligence is the *sine qua non* of leadership. Without it, a person can have the best training in the world, an incisive, analytical mind, and an endless supply of smart ideas, but he still won't make a great leader.[1]

It is also the means by which a leader can sharply increase his/her LSI. In the LSI model, EI is based on resilience, communication and listening skills, happiness, sense of humor, personality traits, assertiveness, flexibility, and empathy in interpersonal interactions. The following sections detail the contributions of each of these components to a leader's emotional intelligence.

RESILIENCE

Resilience is the hallmark of a leader with high EI. But what exactly is resilience? The definitions vary but share the common threads of adaptation, perseverance, and tenacity in the face of stress and/or adversity. Contu said of resilience, "It is merely the skill and the capacity to be robust under conditions of enormous stress and change."[2] For Margolis and Stoltz, "resilience is the capacity to respond quickly and constructively to crises."[3]

Seligman provides this definition based on the combat experience of soldiers. He says:

> How human beings react to extreme adversity is normally distributed. On one end are the people who fall apart into PTSD (Post Traumatic Stress Disorder), depression, and even suicide. In the middle are most people, who at first react with symptoms of depression and anxiety but within a month or so are, by physical and psychological measures, back where they were before the trauma. That is resilience.[4]

Bond and Shapiro reporting on a survey of public and private sector organizational members in the United Kingdom said, "Resilience was defined by most as the ability to recover from setbacks, adapt well to change, and keep going in the face of adversity."[5] One last definition comes from the American Psychological Association (APA), which states, "Resilience is the process of adapting well in the face of adversity, trauma, tragedy, threats or significant sources of stress—such as family and relationship problems, serious health problems or workplace and financial stressors. It means 'bouncing back' from difficult experiences."[6]

A resilient leader then is able to cope with any situation that occurs. He/she controls the situation rather than the situation controlling him/her. As Stoltz put it, "Over the course of your years, either adversity consumes you, or you consume it."[7] Or as Thomas related, "Resilience, a central facet of adaptive capacity, makes it possible for leaders to find calm in the face of tension and to begin the search for answers."[8] But what is the source of a leader's resilience?

Think, for example, of entrepreneur Walt Disney and then imagine a world without Mickey Mouse. But for the resilience of Disney, it could have been. He began his studio career in a venture that ended in bankruptcy just two years after it began. But Disney would not be kept down. He bounced back in the mid-twenties to begin an organization that currently produces over $35 billion per year. And the mouse—Mickey—was inspired by a pet mouse Disney had while working in the previous endeavor that went defunct.[9]

Contu, in discussing the origins of resilience holds that "some people are just born resilient, so the arguments went. There's some truth to that, of course, but an increasing body of empirical evidence shows that resilience—whether in children, survivors of concentration camps, or businesses back from the brink—can be learned."[10] APA says of resilience:

> Resilience is the process of adapting well in the face of adversity, trauma, tragedy, threats or significant sources of stress—such as family and relationship problems, serious health problems or workplace and financial stressors. It means "bouncing back" from difficult experiences.
>
> Research has shown that resilience is ordinary, not extraordinary. People commonly demonstrate resilience. One example is the response of many Americans to the September 11, 2001 terrorist attacks and individuals' efforts to rebuild their lives.
>
> Being resilient does not mean that a person doesn't experience difficulty or distress. Emotional pain and sadness are common in people who have suffered major adversity or trauma in their lives. In fact, the road to resilience is likely to involve considerable emotional distress.
>
> Resilience is not a trait that people either have or do not have. It involves behaviors, thoughts and actions that can be learned and developed in anyone.[11]

Goleman on the topic of resilience stated that "there are two ways to become more resilient: one by talking to yourself, the other by retraining your brain."[12] For dealing with "a major failure" he recommends that you "Talk to yourself. Give yourself a cognitive intervention and counter defeatist thinking with an optimistic attitude. Challenge your downbeat thinking and replace it with a positive outlook."[13]

Retraining your brain, he associates with "more frequent annoying screw-ups, minor setbacks and irritating upsets that are routine in any leader's life."[14]

But he suggests that "Resilience is, again, the answer—but with a different flavor. You need to retrain your brain." And, he expanded that explanation by suggesting developing "mindfulness."[15] According to Goleman 'mindfulness' is "an attention-training method that teaches the brain to register anything happening in the present moment with full focus—but without reacting."[16]

Margolis holds that "we believe that managers can build high levels of resilience in themselves and their teams by taking charge of how they think about adversity."[17] He goes on to state that leaders should develop a "*resilience regimen*" of which he says:

> By asking a series of pointed questions, managers can grasp their own and their direct reports' habits of thought and help reframe negative events in productive ways. With the four lenses as a guide, they can learn to stop feeling paralyzed by crisis, respond with strength and creativity, and help their direct reports do the same.
>
> Resilient managers move quickly from analysis to a plan of action (and reaction). After the onset of adversity, they shift from cause-oriented thinking to response-oriented thinking, and their focus is strictly forward. In our work with leaders in a variety of companies and industries, we've identified four lenses through which managers can view adverse events to make this shift effectively.
>
> *Control.* When a crisis hits, do you look for what you can improve now rather than trying to identify all the factors—even those beyond your control—that caused it in the first place?
>
> *Impact.* Can you sidestep the temptation to find the origins of the problem in yourself or others and focus instead on identifying what positive effects your personal actions might have?
>
> *Breadth.* Do you assume that the underlying cause of the crisis is specific and can be contained, or do you worry that it might cast a long shadow over all aspects of your life?
>
> *Duration.* How long do you believe that the crisis and its repercussions will last?[18]

Seligman, in cooperation with the US Army, has developed a resilience training program called 'master resilience training' (MRT). MRT can be seen as management training—teaching leaders how to embrace resilience and then pass on the knowledge. The content of MRT divides into three parts: building mental toughness, building signature strengths, and building strong relationships.[19]

Resilience then is learnable and teachable. A leader, whatever his/her level of innate resilience, can improve his/her skills in coping/managing events with resilience. And, the display of those skills has an impact on organizational members and through them and the leader, the organization as an entity.

Now a household name, Oprah Winfrey[20] has influenced millions of American women and others across the globe, most probably due to her resolute resilience. Born into a home of poverty to an unwed mother, Oprah was raised to her preteen years by her strong-willed and most influential grandmother. At age six, Oprah was moved to her mother's home in Milwaukee. She was first sexually abused at age nine. This abuse lasted from the ages of nine to thirteen, yet Winfrey's resilience turned her life to one of exceptional giving and support of others. Her network, to date, has raised over $80 million to support and educate children and women.

Resilience in relation to leadership, like many of the characteristics we have discussed, is dichotomous in nature. It is vital that a leader develops and displays resilience, but it is equally vital that a leader imbues his/her organization with a sense of resilience by promoting the development of resilience in organizational members. When organizational members are resilient, the organization is resilient.

Contu, as described earlier, holds that resilient people possess three characteristics, "a staunch acceptance of reality; a deep belief, often buttressed by strongly held values, that life is meaningful; and an uncanny ability to improvise . . . These three characteristics hold true for resilient organizations as well."[21]

Again, based on their survey of organizational members in the United Kingdom, Bond and Shapiro found that the vast majority of people drew their resilience from within citing that "90% of people identified themselves as a source of their own resilience; 52% gave relationships (past and present, both = inside and outside work), with just under half as many again (20%) giving the work they do as a source. But barely 12% of people identified their organisation as a source of resilience."[22]

In contrast, Teixeira and Werther argue that "it is the innovation process and how companies manage it that forms the foundation of a resilient organization."[23] They go on to explain:

> Resilient organizations not only anticipate the needs of buyers but do so by creating an innovation orientation within the firm's culture. This culture-based focus goes beyond any specific innovation; it directs leaders to create an organizational culture that is receptive to innovative ideas and to the changes they produce.
>
> Here, the competitive advantage is not so much innovation per se but the organization's ability to continuously create competitive advantages based on innovations.[24]

In *Building a Resilient Organizational Culture*, Everly argues:

> The key to not only surviving such events, but to prospering during such upheavals, we argue, is human resilience. While human resilience may be thought of

as a personality trait, in the aggregate, groups, organizations, and even communities can learn to develop a "culture of resilience" which manifests itself as a form of "psychological immunity" to, or the ability to rebound from, the untoward effects of adversity.

Our observations have led us to believe that, just as individuals can learn to develop personal traits of resilience, so too can organizations develop a culture of resilience. We would argue that a culture of organizational resilience is built largely upon leadership, what we refer to as "resilient leadership."

We believe key leadership personnel, often frontline leadership, appear to have the ability to "tip" the organization in the direction of resilience and to serve as a catalyst to increase group cohesion and dedication to the "mission." They do this, we argue, by demonstrating four core attributes of optimism, decisiveness, integrity, and open communications while serving as conduits and gatekeepers of formal and informal information flows throughout the organization and enjoying high source credibility (ethos).

All of these can be learned. Simply said, when a small number of high credibility individuals who serve as visible informational channels demonstrate, or "model" the behaviors associated with resilience, we believe they have the ability to change an entire culture of an organization as others replicate the resilient characteristics that they have observed.

As examples of organizational behaviors that promote resilience Everly shares,

- Resilient organizations invest in their client base.
- Resilient organizations are innovative in times of adversity.
- Resilient organizations invest in their leaders.
- Resilient organizations invest in all levels of their workforce.[25]

Whether organizational resilience is based on individual resilience that originates with the individual or is engendered by activities within the organization, organizational resilience is a survival mechanism for an organization and should be cultivated. As Everly states, "Those who cultivate a resilient organization we argue will be better positioned to prosper when others falter."[26] Leaders with high EI and high LSI realize the value of resilience and follow Everly's advice. They cultivate resilience.[27]

COMMUNICATION AND LISTENING

Communication is one of the most powerful tools a leader possesses. In what he/she says and does (not all communication is verbal) a leader establishes the legitimacy of his/her role as a leader. Goleman lists communication as one of the primary social skills of an emotionally intelligent leader, and defines communication as "skill at listening and at sending clear, convincing, and well-tuned messages."[28]

Baldoni says of communication, "Effective communication is not the sole solution to troubled times, but it may be the most effective way to ensure alignment. Listening plays a critical role too. It is well and good to disseminate information, but if you fail to listen to it's echo, that is, how people feel about it as well as understand it, alignment may be doomed."[29] Goleman and Baldoni are correct that both listening and sending messages are vital in communication. And, this emphasis of two-way communication points clearly to the fact that a leader's communication skills must be well-honed, but he/she must also build a communication network based on truth, transparency, and trust.

Listening as a critical skill often does not receive the attention it deserves. Keyser states:

> Successful leaders assert that listening is a key factor to their effectiveness.
>
> These executives actively probe and challenge the information they receive so they can build a strong knowledge base of fresh ideas and insights. Unfortunately, the art of active listening often is overlooked when compared with the other business acumen skills that executives must demonstrate in their day-to-day work and interactions.[30]

Underscoring the importance of listening, Gorysberg and Slind point out, "Leaders who take organizational conversation seriously know when to stop talking and start listening. Few behaviors enhance conversational intimacy as much as attending to what people say. True attentiveness signals respect for people of all ranks and roles, a sense of curiosity, and even a degree of humility."[31] Bommelje's analysis reflects the same theme, "Many leadership and business books indicate that listening is a vital skill. Yet, most people give it little priority."[32] He shares five habits of good listeners that great listeners consistently practice:

1. Find something of interest in the message.
2. Concentrate on content of the message first, and the delivery of it second.
3. Focus on the main point of the message versus just the facts.
4. Take notes, written or mental.
5. Pay genuine attention.[33]

'Active listening' is a term often applied to achieving quality listening skills. According to Bernard Ferrari, dean of the John Hopkins Business School and a well-recognized expert in the field of listening, active listening involves three key practices:[34]

- Show respect—One of the best listeners I have ever observed was the chief operating officer (COO) of a large medical institution. He once told me that he couldn't run an operation as complex as a hospital without seeking input from people at all levels of the staff—from the chief of surgery to the custodial crew. Part of what made him so effective, and so appealing as a manager, was that he let everyone around him know he believed each of them had something unique to contribute. The respect he showed them was reciprocated, and it helped fuel an environment where good ideas routinely came from throughout the institution.

- Keep quiet—I have developed my own variation on the 80/20 rule as it relates to listening. My guideline is that a conversation partner should be speaking 80 percent of the time, while I speak only 20 percent of the time. Moreover, I seek to make my speaking time count by spending as much of it as possible posing questions rather than trying to have my own say.
- Challenge assumptions—Good listeners seek to understand—and challenge—the assumptions that lie below the surface of every conversation.

Good listening skills enable a leader to truly and fully understand and comprehend the information that he/she receives orally. They also are a part of establishing a strong bond of trust when it is obvious to the speaker that the listener is giving the communication his/her undivided attention and respecting what the speaker has to say. These same skills also minimize miscommunication (and the resulting loss of time to revisit the communicator) and productivity when the listener hesitates to act because of uncertainty about the communication.

Clarity of information spoken in communication is vital to what the listener hears. Good speakers, like good writers, realize that clarity, simplicity, focus, brevity, and completeness are essential in communicating the message. These characteristics can be gained through forethought, organization, and plain language or careful selection of words. Furthermore, well-timed presentation with a palpable sense of sincerity and concern for the topic make a huge contribution toward clarity. And finally, and in no small measure, understanding that miscommunication can occur, the effective communicator utilizes feedback mechanisms as well as allowing time for questions.

Tomlinson, in describing the verbal communication skills of effective educational leaders, said:

- They spoke and acted from deep conviction.
- They always remembered the humanity of the people with whom they spoke.
- They listened more than they talked and asked more than they told.
- Their communications and actions cultivated trust.
- What—and how—they communicated helped others develop a sense of agency and competence.

- They asked a great deal from fellow educators—but always provided support so people could reach those high expectations.
- They remembered to express gratitude.[35]

Grossman speaking to the communication skills of business leaders set forth ten communication strategies:

1. "Communicate with integrity, which is all about telling the truth always and without exception because your credibility is at stake," he says.
2. "Make the time to communicate, and make the most of that time," Grossman says.
3. "Remember to answer basic questions employees have"—that is, who, what, where, when, why, and how—"with an emphasis on 'why,'" he says. Too often, leaders "don't share context or rationale or the big picture."
4. Use stories. "The right anecdote can be so much more powerful than theory, fact, or data," he explains.
5. "Build trust and credibility. Be visible, approachable, [and] engage employees in decision-making and key discussions."
6. "Hold a mirror up to yourself," Grossman says. "Consider how you would like to be communicated with if you're in employees' shoes."
7. "Outline expectations clearly, so employees know what you expect of them."
8. "Don't wait to communicate until you have all the answers."
9. "Provide context and relevance, which allows employees to get at the meaning, the rationale, and understand what it means to them."
10. "Be human and empathetic, and show you care."[36]

Poor communication whether in sending information or when listening can be as disruptive and potentially destructive as high-quality communication is beneficial. Solomon reports that "91% of employees say communication issues can drag executives down, according to results from our new Interact/Harris Poll."[37] Communication mistakes or errors can take many forms. Grossman[38] suggests that leaders should avoid these common communication mistakes that can get in the way of your business:

- Inconsistent or mixed messages
- Talking at someone instead of with them
- Delays in communication—not responding quickly in order to wait to share "all" the information at once
- "Spinning" messages instead of speaking truthfully
- Not telling the truth (or silence)

- Using language, jargon, or terms that others don't understand
- Not allowing people to feel heard
- Not really listening to what people are saying—and not saying—to you
- Speaking too quickly or talking too much
- Using negative body language
- Using only logic without emotion, or using only emotion without logic
- Failing to ask people what they think, thereby ensuring that you were understood correctly
- Too much communication—an overabundance of communication, constantly checking in on people and inundating them with calls, or emails, for example, might be construed by some as annoying, or worse, that you don't trust them[39]

Written communication is another area where the skills of the writer (speaker/sender) and the reader (the receiver/reader) impact the transmission of information. If you have ever received a report, memo, or e-mail that is chock full of typos, misspellings, poor sentence structure, and/or that is lacking in general written structure you know what that does to communication.

The goal of any written business communication should be clarity gained via logical sequence and readability, simplicity gained through clear expression of thoughts and ideas, focus gained by staying on topic, brevity gained through the parsimonious use of words, and completeness based on inclusion of needed information. As Weeks shares, "business readers are content driven, time pressed, and in search of solutions." She offers the following suggestions for writers:

- First, they should get out of the impressive-language business. To content-driven readers, language simply carries information, ideas, and the relationships among them.
- Second, organization is critical. Whatever particular analysis you make or actions you advocate, how compelling readers will find your report or memo depends largely on how logically you order and present information and ideas.[40]

To maximize the impact of her suggestions, she offers these strategies:

From your introduction the content-driven reader judges whether the rest of your memo is worth his time. Yet the beginning is where many writers ease in and build slowly. This is a mistake. Your opening must answer the reader's question "Why am I reading this?" To do so, it needs to establish the relevance and the utility of the document as a whole. (To establish relevance she recommends the following based on the work of Barbara Minto in the book *The Minto Pyramid Principle: Logic in Writing, Thinking and Problem Solving*.)

The situation: A quick, factual sketch of the current business situation that serves to anchor the reader

The complication: A problem that unsettles the situation in the story you're telling. It's why you're writing the memo or report.

The question: This might be "What should we do?" "How can we do it?" or "What's wrong with what we tried?" The question does not necessarily have to be spelled out; it may be implied.

The answer: Your response to the question and your solution to the complication.

The order in which the elements appear can vary.

Put the weight at the front of each section. Readers like the journalistic approach—even if the story will break the hearts of millions, journalists give it away in the headline.

Use reader-oriented judgment to decide the right level of detail. Many over-writers pride themselves on their thoroughness, while underwriters congratulate themselves for being admirably brief. Both do a disservice to their readers and hence to themselves. Over-writers risk losing readers in a flood of detail, while underwriters may come across as superficial thinkers. From the reader's point of view, thorough means "exhaustive" and brief means "short"; the goal should be to be concise, which means "as tight as possible, but complete."

Write well and the message is communicated effectively and productivity results. Write poorly and the message is lost and productivity suffers. What might also suffer is the image of the writer as a competent individual and the reputation of the organization may suffer as well.

The universal view of the importance of communication and listening adds even more credibility to the time worn notion that "leaders should always be mindful that what they say and 'how' they say it" as that has impact. A sharp quip or a too-sudden negative reply can do untold harm professionally and personally as both elicit an emotional reaction and probably a negative one. It is situations such as this where EI plays a critical intervening role. Effective communication is about getting the point across in a positive nonthreatening manner, with EI this can be done by applying leadership intelligence.

HAPPINESS

FDR was a man who could have been bitter. Struck with polio in 1921, Roosevelt had enjoyed a previously healthy life. At the age of thirty-nine, he lost the use of his legs and much of his bowel function. Yet, FDR had a positive spirit, a happy outlook and a charming manner. In 1932, this man overwhelmingly beat Herbert Hoover for the seat of the presidency.[41]

Happiness is an internal, emotional state of mind. It is that place and point in time where consciously, in a reflective moment, but more often unconsciously, an individual is at peace with himself/herself and is at peace with the people and daily events in his/her life. He/she is satisfied and enjoys a sense of wholeness, comfort, and well-being.

Denier, an early researcher in the field of subjective well-being or happiness, related:

> The area of subjective well-being has three hallmarks. First, it is subjective. Second, subjective well-being includes positive measures. It is not just the absence of negative factors, as is true of most measures of mental health. Third, the subjective well-being measures typically include a global assessment of all aspects of a person's life. Although affect or satisfaction within a certain domain may be assessed, the emphasis is usually placed on an integrated judgment of the person's life.[42]

Put simply, happiness is an individual characteristic and can only be assessed by the individual himself/herself. Furthermore, happiness for any individual is based on the totality of his/her life circumstance. However, happiness or satisfaction with any one aspect of a person's life such as his/her work can be assessed, although the assessment is still subjective and applies only to that individual.

Daskal, described happiness succinctly and eloquently when she said, "We talk about happiness as if it were a thing to be discovered and acquired. But happiness can never be found externally. It is not a possession to be acquired or a set of conditions, but a state of mind."[43] Taking the broadest possible view, happy people tend to be better satisfied with both their personal and professional lives than unhappy people. It is that sense of satisfaction with their job, the work he/she performs as a leader, and satisfaction of organizational members with the work they individually perform that is a prime concern for the emotionally intelligent leader.

Individual happiness as a leader is more than not dreading to go to work in the morning or the sense of accomplishment when a solitary goal or set of goals is met, though at times meeting one specific goal or set of goals may generate momentary happiness or satisfaction. That type of happiness is transitory at best but does add to the cumulative sum of events and interactions that create and sustain happiness and satisfaction over time. Daskal states that "the happiest people don't necessarily have the best of everything, but they have learned to make the best of whatever they have. The happiest leaders aren't necessarily focused on success or failure but live by a different perspective—and that outlook makes all the difference."[44] She outlines ten characteristics that exemplify happy leaders:

1. Their life has purpose and meaning.
2. They concentrate on positive thoughts.
3. They judge their wins and failures the same.
4. They prioritize what's important.
5. They don't compare themselves with others.
6. They cultivate meaningful relationships.
7. They invest in diversity.
8. They're constantly growing.
9. They do what they say they're going to do.
10. They believe in themselves.[45]

Research shows as well that leader happiness positively impacts organizational member performance. In a meta-analysis the relationship between leader trait affectivity (happiness) and several leadership criteria, Joseph et al. found that "leader trait affectivity, particularly leader trait positive affect, plays a significant role in predicting leadership criteria."[46]

In her study of how leader happiness and sadness influence follower performance Visser et al. found that "leaders were perceived as more effective when displaying happiness rather than sadness."[47] Leader happiness alone, however, is not sufficient to drive an enterprise.

Leaders must strive to create conditions that allow organizational members to achieve happiness/satisfaction in their work. As Spreitzer and Porath share, "Happy employees produce more than unhappy ones over the long term. They routinely show up at work, they're less likely to quit, they go above and beyond the call of duty, and they attract people who are just as committed to the job. Moreover, they're not sprinters; they're more like marathon runners, in it for the long haul."[48]

Martin holds that "Employees are the backbone of any organization, and as you might expect, studies show that happy employees are more motivated, productive and committed."[49] He goes on to suggest that there are three "community-related drivers of happiness" (community is his term for the work place). The first feature that drives happiness is one's perceived value in the eyes of the relevant community.

The second feature of consequence is how much one values the community in question. The third feature of happiness is equally interrelated: the degree to which the community is valued by others outside of it.[50] Of these drivers of organization member happiness, he shares:

A leader who aims to nurture employee happiness must develop operating systems and a culture that reinforce the role of the individual within the context of the community. If each individual employee is unaware of what community they are a part, and how that community measures their value as a member, the firm will be incapable of being a positive force in helping the individual be happy as a member of the firm. He or she may be happy, but their happiness will derive from sources outside of the firm, and he or she will not give the firm any credit for their sense of well-being.

In order for individuals to relate to communities within a firm, there have to be communities to relate to. Leaders should view their firm as a nested set of communities, with individuals as the key components of each. Hence, the nurturing of communities—both sub-segments of the firm such as work-groups or divisions and the overall community of the firm—is a key task for business leaders.[51]

Emotionally intelligent leaders have an advantage in deriving work/career-related happiness themselves and in creating conditions, as Martin espouses, that offer the opportunity for organizational members to find meaning and happiness in what they do. Knowing yourself well enough as a leader to follow a course that leads to your individual fulfillment while knowing the members of your organization well enough to create conditions for them that allow the same fulfillment is emblematic of a leader with high leadership intelligence.

SENSE OF HUMOR

Dwight D. Eisenhower, former president of the United States, is credited with saying "A sense of humor is part of the art of leadership, of getting along with people, of getting things done."[52] He was right across the board. Leadership, like teaching, is art applied scientifically. And, two of the primary character-istics of a great leader are the ability to get along with people and being able to get things done. Eisenhower's quip is supported by research.

As Sala shared, "More than four decades of study by various researchers confirms some common-sense wisdom: Humor, used skillfully, greases the management wheels. It reduces hostility, deflects criticism, relieves tension, improves morale, and helps communicate difficult messages."[53] Similarly, a study by the Bell Leadership Group found that "when employees are asked to describe the strengths and weaknesses of senior colleagues in their organiza-tions, 'sense of humor' and 'work ethic' are mentioned twice as much as any other phrases."[54]

Based on a study of leader humor styles, Unal concluded that "this study supports the assumption that self-enhancing humor employed by leaders may play an important role in enhancing employees' job related affective well-being."[55] In a meta-analysis of the literature related to sense of humor Brooks shared that "it is concluded that humor is a useful, but delicate, communica-tion tool for leaders."[56]

It is the 'delicate' nature of humor that a leader must be acutely aware of Sala shares the following:

> In 1998, research by the Hay Group and Daniel Goleman found that superior leaders share a set of emotional-intelligence characteristics, chief among them high self-awareness and an exceptional ability to empathize. These qualities are critical to managers' effective use of humor. They can make the difference between the pitch-perfect zinger and the barb that just stings.
>
> But the point is not that more humor is always good or that positive humor is always better than negative, disparaging humor. In business, as in life, the key to the effective use of humor is how it's deployed. Don't try to be funny. But do pay closer attention to how you use humor, how others respond to your humor, and the messages you send. It's all in the telling.[57]

In like reference:

> The Bell study also looked at the specific ways in which senior managers use humor to improve performance. The most effective leaders use humor to spark people's enthusiasm, deliver an honest message in a good-natured way, boost productivity, put people at ease, bring teams together, and see the light side of a situation. Less effective leaders use humor in negative ways—to show off, cut people down with sarcasm, and overly distract people from the task at hand.[58]

Craumar shares this about the use of humor:

> As a rule, avoid any attempts at humor that are hurtful or offensive, or would make others feel uncomfortable. Jokes about religion, politics, or body functions are bound to offend someone. Sexual innuendo is another no-no as is any joke that makes fun of someone's appearance. Racist or ethnic humor is also unacceptable. And humor should never make light of your people's issues or concerns.[59]

Romero and Cruthirds express their concern about the use of humor saying "it can be perceived as humorous by one person yet quite offensive to another person. Consequently, humor can result in a negative and/or positive effect for the individuals involved in a humorous exchange. Additionally, unwanted humor can cause problems in organizations."[60]

Tobak in commentary for CNS News shared the following about sense of humor:

> So, assuming your sense of humor is of the appropriate kind, here are 7 reasons why I think it's one of the most underrated leadership traits:
>
> 1. *Humor is disarming.* It lightens the mood, puts people at ease and cuts down on the intimidation factor that powerful leaders face with employees, customers, vendors, partners, everyone. It shows you don't take yourself too seriously. That's the humility factor.

2. *It relieves tension during crises.* In the corporate world, I'd say that most managers and executives face a tough situation at least weekly. When there's tension in the room, it helps you and your employees to relax, think more clearly, and make better decisions.

3. *It softens the blow of bad news.* Don't get me wrong; if you're announcing layoffs you probably don't want to lead with "Two employees walk into a bar . . ." That said, success is a poor teacher; we learn more from failure. But you still need someone to smile and say, "Hey, life goes on, we'll win next time. Now let's all go get a drink."

4. *Humor is great for team building.* For some reason, when a team laughs and has fun together it facilitates a sense of community and helps to create a cohesive corporate culture. It also helps to create a sort of communal history, as in, "Remember the time when . . ."

5. *It gets people to root for you.* People like folks with a sense of humor. They're more likely to want you to succeed. Your supporters will find you more likeable and your detractors will be more likely to cut you some slack.

6. *It places emphasis on key points.* People remember stories. Dramatic anecdotes, including the comedic kind, resonate with folks.

7. *Humor is motivating.* As executives go, I wasn't really the nicest guy you'd want to work for, but I think people learned and accomplished a great deal and had some fun doing it. I could be wrong, but I think the sense of humor helped to keep folks motivated, especially when times were hard.[61]

Emotional intelligence and common sense are the keys to applying humor effectively in the work place and in reality in any setting. But, as Craumer shares about using humor in the work place:

> If it doesn't fit your personality, don't try. Nothing is more painful than watching an earnest or desperate attempt at humor fail miserably. Just ask any stand-up comedian who's bombed on stage. You don't have to be the source of humor—just create the conditions in which humor can flourish. The key is to find your own parameters of comfort and work within them.[62]

That rare individual leader who seems to lack a sense of humor or who struggles with humorous quips should follow Craumer's advice. Creating conditions that allow the proper use of humor minimize the risk of being seen as too stoic or humorless. But those who take the risk of applying their sense of humor have a potential reward of greater engagement and productivity. Leaders with high LSI can make that judgment correctly.

PERSONALITY TRAITS

A person is defined by their individual personality. Like a fingerprint, it is theirs and theirs alone. Personality is what makes each of us who we are.

It also defines to a great extent our interaction with others. Psychological research provides us a clear schematic of the attributes of personality in the five-factor model.

A full recitation of the development of the five-factor model is beyond the scope of this discussion. However, based on the work of William McDouglall, Tupes and Christal, Cattell, Digman, and many others, a consensus as to the predominate traits from which personality forms and finds expression has been developed and is widely accepted. As Digman shared in 1990, "the past decade has witnessed a rapid convergence of views regarding the structure of the concepts of personality (i.e. the language of personality)."[63]

It now appears quite likely that what Norman (1963) offered many years ago as an effort 'toward an adequate taxonomy for personality attributes' has matured into a theoretical structure of surprising generality, with stimulating links to psycholinguistics and cross-cultural psychology, cognitive theory, and other areas of psychology. McCrea and John came to a similar conclusion about the five-factor model saying, "Research using both natural language adjectives and theoretically based personality questionnaires supports the comprehensiveness of the model and its applicability across observers and cultures."[64]

The five-factor model rests on the tenet that the attributes of "extraversion/ introversion (or surgency), friendliness/hostility (or agreeableness), conscientiousness (or will), neuroticism/emotional stability (or emotional stability), and intellect (or openness)" are the primary factors that determine personality.[65] Even with consensus on the importance of these factors, of course, there still remains substantial debate as to whether or to what extent personality is inherited or developed/learned, the nature or nurture conundrum and the extent/weight of the contribution of each factor to the personality of any given individual.

That conundrum and consideration of the importance of each factor is beyond the scope of this discussion as well. Nonetheless, the five-factor model forms the basis of our considerations regarding personality, emotional intelligence, and LSI.

The emergence and acceptance of the five-factor model has prompted a large amount of research examining the relationship between the five factors and various aspects of the work environment.

As might be anticipated the results differ somewhat but generally indicate that all or some of the personality attributes of the five-factor model are related to leadership behavior. In a study of leader personality and assessment of leader behavior, Bergman et al. report that "analysis showed that the Big Five variables were significantly related to the managers' leadership behavior in all CPE dimensions."[66] The change, production, employee (CPE) instrument is a 360-degree instrument. In the CPE instrument, "leadership behavior is rated on 24 items in three different dimensions: change, production, and employee orientation."[67]

Kornør found that "the strongest predictors of the CPE total score were Conscientiousness and Extraversion."[68] Chi, in a study of negative emotional leadership displays, shared that "our findings suggest that leader negative emotional expression is positively related to the performance of conscientious and agreeable followers. When these kinds of followers do not perform well on their tasks, leaders could display *moderate levels* of negative emotions during performance feedback sessions, as conscientious and agreeable followers are able to process such negative social information and take actions to address the cause of such information.

However, it should be noted that we are not contending that 'expressing negative emotions' is always a good choice for leaders; rather, we suggest that this might lead to higher performance for certain types of followers."[69] Kalshoven examined the relationship between the five-factor model and ethical leadership. Her results indicated "conscientiousness and agreeableness were most consistently related to ethical leadership."[70]

Kempke Eppler, in a study of the relationship between the five-factor model, attributes and organizational culture found "a significant correlation between the market cultural value and extraversion, agreeableness, and emotional stability."[71] By examining the relationship between leader-member exchange (LMX) and span of control, Schyns et al. found that "extraversion, conscientiousness, and agreeableness moderate the relationship between span of control and various dimensions of LMX."[72]

Judge and Bono share that "results based on 14 samples of leaders from over 200 organizations revealed that Extraversion and Agreeableness positively predicted transformational leadership."[73] Finally, in a recent meta-analysis of how personality factors impact management team decision making, Abatecola et al. found that "firm performance seems to be positively affected by CEO emotional stability, which also impacts on the strategic pro-activity of firms, as well as CEO extraversion and conscientiousness. Furthermore, CEO conscientiousness seems also associated with the bureaucratization of the firm organizational structure."[74]

The studies cited highlight two conclusions. First, personality is related to leadership. A leader's personality will/can either enhance his/her performance in a specific organization or cause the leader to derail in that organization. It is a matter of fit and of the leader's flexibility. Second, leader emotional intelligence can mitigate circumstances and allow a leader to exert his/her LSI, or as Maccorby related:

> I have found that there are four concepts that are particularly useful to understanding people and predict how they are likely to behave at work. They are:

1. Talents and Temperament—what we are born with
2. Social character—how we are like others brought up in the same culture
3. Personality type—how we are like some people within our culture
4. Identities—how we want to define ourselves

These different concepts are windows on the self—the person—and include values, emotional attitudes, characteristic ways of working and relating to others, the identities we give to ourselves, and our ways of acquiring, retaining, and transforming information.

Talent and temperament includes intelligence and creative gifts. Psychologists do agree that there are five genetically influenced personality traits that can be observed from infancy on. These traits, called the Big Five, are:

1. Openness to experience and curiosity versus just following the same routine. This trait has become especially valuable in companies that must adapt to a changing market.
2. Agreeableness versus suspiciousness. The most effective leaders attract people and are only suspicious of those who betray their trust.
3. Emotional stability versus emotional instability is clearly a quality that protects a person from being overwhelmed by inevitable setbacks.
4. Conscientiousness, sticking with a task, versus being easily distracted—a quality shared by all successful people.
5. Extraversion, sociability versus introversion, does not, in my experience, predict success or failure. Both qualities can be useful. Typically, effective salespeople are extroverts and strategists tend to be introverts.

Social Character is a concept that connects personality and culture. It is that part of personality shaped by family, school, sports, and workplace, so that we have the emotional attitudes and values that equip us to succeed in a particular culture with its dominant mode of production.

Personality types describe variations within a social character.

Identities (are) how we want to define ourselves.[75]

Of identities Maccorby shares, "An effective leader recognizes personality differences, but succeeds in creating a common sense of purpose, a shared identity as members of a team."[76]

A leader who is reflective about his/her personality and the personalities of those he/she works with may have what Maccorby calls personality intelligence, of which he says:

Understanding personality has become essential for leaders of the complex, knowledge-base companies operating in the global marketplace. This imperative has been made even more challenging by the need for managers to recognize that many of the personalities they must understand were formed in different cultures with different attitudes to authority. Otherwise, managers will risk losing the trust of the people they lead. Today, in order to fit people into the right roles, leaders need to develop what I call Personality Intelligence.[77]

Such intelligence is related to emotional intelligence in the LSI model and is one more aspect of leadership about which a leader must be cognizant.

ASSERTIVENESS

From a leadership perspective, to move an organization forward one must assert themselves. Learning how to be assertive in an effective manner is based in large part on a leader's ability to gauge the existing emotional situation and emotional impact of his/her actions. Santora stated that "one of the characteristics that people sometimes look for in leaders is assertiveness. But where should leaders draw the line when it comes to assertiveness?"[78] Santora based his answer on the results of a study by Ames and Flynn who found:

> The present research confirmed our expectation that individual differences in assertiveness are a critical component of perceptions of leadership and that the link between assertiveness and leadership is not as simple as was suggested by prior reports of positive or negative linear effects. References to assertiveness dominated perceptions about the weaknesses of potential leaders, having appeared as a clear theme in as many as half of the coworker comments, far more frequently than references to other commonly studied attributes, including intelligence, conscientiousness, and charisma.[79]

Put more simply, leaders who display moderate levels of assertiveness are more well accepted than those at either extreme who are overly assertive or lack assertiveness.

Still, as Edinger says, "If I had to pick one skill for the majority of leaders I work with to improve, it would be assertiveness. Not because being assertive is such a wonderful trait in and of itself. Rather, because of its power to magnify so many other leadership strengths."[80] Edinger goes on to share specific ways that assertiveness can complement critical leadership skills someone already possesses:

- Creating a culture of innovation
- Being customer focused
- Fostering teamwork and collaboration
- Leading change
- Acting with integrity

- Creating a safe environment
- Communicating effectively.[81]

Assertiveness, though, has another aspect, one related to Edinger's point that appropriate assertiveness is a leadership expectation. But, assertiveness is also about how a leader approaches conflict. It is easy to assume that a leader by one means or another will exert his/her will and more pointedly so when challenged. As Ames says:

> Assertiveness is a characterization of how a person responds in a situation in which her positions and/or interests are, or could be, in conflict with others' positions or interests. That is, given some real or potential opposition, people must repeatedly grapple with a basic question: How hard should I push? I believe peoples' behavioral responses to this question are generally arrayed in the minds of both actors and observers along a dimension ranging from avoidance and passivity at one extreme to aggression and hostility at the other.[82]

This reflects the point made earlier, that a leader must learn how to assert himself/herself in an effective manner and that doing so involves being able to gauge the existing emotional situation and emotional impact of his/her actions—to be assertive enough without being overly assertive, to be in a word "emotionally intelligent" and exercise LSI.

FLEXIBILITY

In juxtaposition to assertiveness is flexibility. The constant flux of any enterprise calls for leaders to be flexible. As Good and Sharma share, "Leader flexibility can be a pivotal aspect of leadership development."[83] In the same vein, Yukl states that "research on leadership and management during the past several decades provide strong evidence that flexible, adaptive leadership is essential for most managers."[84]

But what constitutes flexibility? Aaker and Mascarenhas provide the classic definition: flexibility represents the "ability of the organization to adapt to substantial, uncertain and fast occurring (relative to the required reaction time) environmental changes that have a meaningful impact on the organization's performance."[85] Other, more recent definitions describe flexibility in terms of adaptability. Soffer says, "Basically, flexibility is described as capability to react to uncertainty by adaptation."[86]

Likewise Calarco shared that "adaptability—responding effectively to change—has become recognized as a necessary skill for leaders of all kinds of organizations."[87] Schultz describes flexibility as "Agility—being able to rapidly adapt to disruptive forces and competitive challenges—is the goal of many enterprises."[88]

Other aspects of flexibility include a willingness to allow broad latitude in decision-making and allowing latitude to employees in their work schedule. Benjaafar cites that "Marshack and Nelson suggested flexibility be viewed as a mechanism which allows decision makers to take advantage of future information. They conjectured that the greater the current uncertainty and/or the greater the expected amount of future information the more important is flexibility."[89] Of the latter, Behson says, "If properly managed, with an eye towards effective job redesign, flexibility can also enhance performance."[90] Adaptability and agility in the face of change then are the primary characteristics of flexibility. And as the definitions show, flexibility is not a singular construct but a multivariate construct that is variable based on situation and need. Good and Sharma suggest nine areas of flexibility:

- Coping flexibility—It is defined in the context of stressful life situations. It involves variation in the appraisal of the situation and variation in the strategy employed to cope with it (Cheng, 2001).
- Explanatory flexibility—It relates to how well one varies the appraisal of the cause of events (Silverman and Peterson, 1993; Moore and Fresco, 2007).
- Interpersonal flexibility—Leaders interact with multiple stakeholders and must continually vary behavior both within and across different interpersonal engagements (Hall et al., 1998).
- Emotional flexibility—It is the ability to regulate emotions across different situations (Rozanski and Kubzansky, 2005).
- Learning flexibility—Given the unpredictable and ever-changing contexts faced by leaders, they may have to change their preferred style of learning in order to meet the demands of the situation.
- Communication flexibility—Leaders often communicate visions that both inspire and set forth clear expectations (Kotter, 1996). Given the dynamic environment that leaders operate in, such goals, expectations, and even the audience may be continually shifting, requiring the leader to change his/her communication along with the situation.
- Gender flexibility—The capacity and willingness to be flexible in adopting traditionally masculine, as well as feminine, traits are essential to leadership (Cann and Siegfried, 1990).
- Cognitive flexibility—Complexity brought forth by continuous change creates a context in which issues are increasingly ill-defined (Jacques, 1989; Mumford and Connelly, 1991). This not only requires creative problem solving to react to changes (Mumford et al., 2000), but also the capacity and willingness to proactively construe a given context from a fundamentally

diverse perspective (Runco, 1994). A leader must be able to notice and create new ideas regardless of the changing situation rather than becoming stuck in a singular method of response (Mumford and Connelly, 1991; Scratchley and Hakstian, 2001).
• Decision-making flexibility—Decision making is an important aspect of leadership (Vroom and Yetton, 1973). To be an effective decision-maker, the leader should generate alternatives that deal with change reactively and proactively.[91]

The characteristics of adaptability and agility apply to all forms of flexibility, including the flexibility of the leader himself/herself; the flexibility of the leader in interaction with others; and organizational flexibility. Hannah et al. describe the first form of leader flexibility as the self-construct of which he says, "Leaders' positive self-conceptions have been recognized as important factors in influencing this (positive human cognitions, affects, goals and values, expectancies, and self-regulatory plans) positivity. Further, leaders who, in their self-construct, are oriented toward growth and the fulfillment of human potential are more likely to bring about these same outcomes in those they lead."[92] Essentially a leader must know himself/herself well and recognize the importance of flexibility to accommodate flexibility individually and to allow/promote flexibility for organizational members and through them the organization as a whole.

Flexibility in interaction with others, Goleman holds, is related to a leader's mastery of multiple leadership styles. Goleman describes six leadership styles: coercive style, authoritative style, affiliative style, democratic style, pacesetting style, and coaching style.[93] According to Goleman, "the most effective leaders switch flexibly among the leadership styles as needed."[94] He states in description of such flexible leaders that "they are exquisitely sensitive to the impact they are having on others and seamlessly adjust their style to get the best results."[95]

By shifting between styles as needed the leader displays his/her flexibility and simultaneously signals to organizational members that flexibility is acceptable. Organizational flexibility is based not only on leader and members' flexibility but also on the general characteristics of the organization as an entity. Akdemir et al. enumerated twenty-six characteristics of high-performance (flexible) organizations:

1. Well-understood vision and values
2. Flexibility and proper use of discipline
3. Set clear and specific goals
4. Strong communication
5. Trust and confidence

6. Fun
7. Decision making at the lowest level
8. Effective training
9. Performance feedback
10. A stronger, more consistent customer focus and total quality
11. Multiple methods of measuring improvement
12. Strategic change management
13. Encouragement of innovation and openness to technology
14. Team-based work
15. Participative leadership
16. Effective incentive system
17. Recruiting and hiring the best talent
18. Work-life balance
19. Workplace diversity
20. Motivation
21. Compensation and performance appraisal
22. Knowledge management
23. Meaningful job
24. Effective succession planning
25. Effective planning and analysis
26. Ethical decision making and peer respect[96]

The leader of such an organization would be very flexible and would exhibit the characteristic of a Level 5 leader as described by Collins. "Individuals do not need to proceed sequentially through each level of the hierarchy to reach the top, but to be a full-fledged Level 5 requires the capabilities of all the lower levels, plus the special characteristics of Level 5."[97]

- Level 5 executive builds enduring greatness through a paradoxical combination of personal humility plus professional will.
- Level 4 effective leader catalyzes commitment to and vigorous pursuit of a clear and compelling vision; stimulates the group to high-performance standards.
- Level 3 competent manager organizes people and resources toward the effective and efficient pursuit of predetermined objectives.
- Level 2 contributing team member contributes to the achievement of group objectives; works effectively with others in a group setting.
- Level 1 highly capable individual makes productive contributions through talent, knowledge, skills, and good work habits.

Only when organizational members know that a leader can be both constructively assertive and yet flexible are they at ease with a leader. As Good and Sharma share, "Leader flexibility can be a pivotal aspect of leadership development."[98] Such a leader also displays LSI in arriving at the decision that flexibility builds individuals and organization.

EMPATHY/INTERPERSONAL INTERACTIONS

On occasion, we hear of a person described as "a cold fish" denoting a lack of appropriate emotional response. Scientifically, based on severity, this condition is termed 'reduced, negative, or incongruent affect display.' Psychologically, "affective display is defined as behavior which acts as a sign of emotion which can be seen visually in the manner it is displaced, such as facial expressions, vocally expressed feelings, or gestures like mannerisms or body language."[99]

Reduced, negative, or incongruent affective display occurs when a person fails to respond in a normal way to an event or circumstance. A normal response might be, for example, smiling when hearing an amusing story and scowling or frowning when hearing an untoward remark. Another example of a normal response would be expressing enjoyment or pleasure when a sought after goal is achieved or expressing concern when a troubling issue is brought to light.

Contrast those normal responses with the responses of 'a cold fish.' A reduced, negative or incongruent response might be, for example, not smiling when hearing an amusing story or failing to react when hearing an untoward remark. Another example of a reduced, negative, or incongruent response would be failure to express enjoyment or pleasure when a sought after goal is achieved or failure to express concern when a troubling issue is brought to light.

Individuals who lack empathy and struggle with interpersonal interaction are often viewed negatively, that is as having affective issues. In a study of the impact of incongruent affective behavior, Szczurek et al. shared about the finding of their study, "these findings shed light on the importance of affective displays in social interaction and personal perception. These demonstrate how one's subtle departures from normative affect can result in being disliked and avoided, eliciting outrage and a suspicion that one's moral values are misaligned from those of the observer."[100] The point is that a leader needs to display a positive aspect. As Goleman stated, "A leader needs to make sure that not only is he regularly in an optimistic, authentic, high-energy mood, but also that, through his chosen actions, his followers feel and act that way, too."[101]

Ronald Reagan was such a man.[102] Although not a picky eater, there were a few things he did not like. Ever the empathic, Reagan kept his food dislikes a secret as he didn't want to offend farmers who raised those crops to be alienated by others.

But how does a leader display empathy? Goleman says:

> Empathy doesn't mean a kind of "I'm okay, you're okay" mushiness. For a leader, that is, it doesn't mean adopting other people's emotions as one's own and trying to please everybody. That would be a nightmare-it would make action impossible. Rather, empathy means thoughtfully considering employees' feelings—along with other factors-in the process of making intelligent decisions. Empathy is particularly important today as a component of leadership for at least three reasons: the increasing use of teams; the rapid pace of globalization; and the growing need to retain talent.[103]

Wilson shared about empathy:

> Empathy isn't everything, however. Just adding a dose of empathy to Bezos's cereal in the morning won't do the trick. We heard again and again that business leaders want executives at every level to have the whole package—all five Third Space attributes. You can be disposed toward empathy, but incompetent at exercising it if you lack the cultural competence to pick up on cues in your surroundings, the intellectual curiosity to explore other people's reality, the 360-degree thinking to see all the way around a situation, or the adaptability to accommodate what you have come to understand. But empathy remains an emotional foundation—it's the "attribute-prime" of successful leaders.[104]

Badea shared:

> Empathy is the ability to get an insight or recognize the emotions of others. Empathy does not mean that we live emotions of other people, but it means that we understand other people's emotions from our experiences.[105]

Dwight D. Eisenhower could have been the poster child for empathy.[106] In spite of the fact that he *commanded* the troops, Eisenhower felt a genuine tenderness for his men. He realized and acknowledged the very real, individual ramifications of the decisions he made on each one of them. In Eisenhower's case, his empathy fueled his leadership excellence and his ability to successfully command. Because of his empathy, those under his authority had a great respect and sense of allegiance toward him. They knew he would not make a decision involving their welfare unless he believed it was absolutely necessary.

In the LSI model, empathy is also the gateway to strong interpersonal relationships. Leaders by definition have followers (for leaders this means organizational members and/or consumers of the product or service the organization produces/offers). Research has shown with some clarity that leaders who are able to establish a firm bond of trust and respect with both internal and external constituencies of an organization produce positive results.

Warren Bennis said it this way, "great leaders earn respect, daily, and build and maintain trust with all constituents."[107] Emotional intelligence promotes the development of trust and respect through leader display of empathy in the interpersonal interactions that make up the majority of the work in his/her routine day. A leader with high LSI will also display high emotional intelligence.

EMOTIONAL INTELLIGENCE AND LEADERSHIP

The emergence of emotional intelligence as a prime driving force in leadership gives added emphasis to the importance of soft skills described to this point that support credibility, competence, inspiration, and vision. People are rational but also emotional beings. They often react as much or more with their hearts as they do with their minds. The leader who, through developing his/her leadership intelligence, can also master the ability to recognize and react appropriately to both the rational and emotional sides of an individual has a decided advantage over he leader who lacks those abilities. When, in addition, a leader has a firm grasp of his/her own rational and emotional sides he/she greatly expands the likelihood of success for himself/herself, the individuals within the organization and the organization itself.

Part III

TRUE NORTH LEADERSHIP
PERSONALIZED

Chapter 8

'Updating Your Internal GPS'
Building Leadership Intelligence

As you may have discerned at this point, some or perhaps several of the Leadership Intelligence (LSI) constructs you are already comfortable with or are relatively familiar to you. Similarly, as a driver, there are places you regularly 'go' for which you need no assistance. For these trips as well as local ones around town, you may never need to engage your GPS. Once you learn a route, it can become second nature, practically like turning on 'auto-pilot' to return to this destination.

Similarly, in those LSI components in which you are confident, you simply continue to move forward with 'map' updates as needed. However, with the realization that you may need additional information in some area, you might—in a metaphorical sense—decide to engage the GPS for assistance.

Analogously, for all leaders, even those with seemingly innate leadership ability, LSI must be occasionally updated. This is the result of training, imprinting (hopefully in an organization with leaders who excel), and active learning in all situations. It is a coming together of skills that can be learned. LSI must also be constantly reinforced and broadened in depth and scope as changes occur in the circumstances of the leader, the organization of which he/she is a part, and the environment (the global world) in which the organization exists.

The primary rationale for building LSI is that the aspiring leader be open to learning; learning as a student while in post-secondary education or perhaps earlier, and learning on the job when he/she enters the work world. Without that predisposition, development of LSI will be slow and the progress toward mastery of the skills related to LSI will be sporadic at best. In addition to being open to learning, the aspiring leader must actively seek out learning opportunities.

Having a mentor is one such opportunity. As Bennis points out regarding mentoring, "The best mentors are usually recruited, and one mark of a future leader is the ability to identify, woo, and win the mentors who will change his or her life."[1] Bennis' point is well taken. Everyone has been around people who have knowledge that would be beneficial to others. But how many have taken the time to seek out or create opportunities for those individuals to share the knowledge they have?

The inquisitive, curious, and determined (one might say 'dogged'), among those new to a field of endeavor (or even those long term in a field who want to expand their horizons), may be a step ahead. They establish relationships with peers and superiors that allow them access to the knowledge they seek and the learning opportunities that knowledge brings. Without necessarily calling them mentors, they have established a mentoring relationship.

Another learning opportunity is found through imprinting. This type of learning occurs in a different manner than mentoring. Imprinting occurs during a sensitive period when an individual first joins an organization or when he/she moves to a different position within that organization or even to another organization. It occurs through observation and/or interaction with others within the organization. Put simply, aspiring leaders are imprinted individually with skills and dispositions exhibited by those organizational leaders and peers.

And, that imprinting is reflective of the knowledge and practices within that organization in general. This type of learning is heuristic in nature, occurring as the observer attempts to make sense of the steps taken to answer a question or reach a goal or objective. And, unlike mentoring, it may not involve direct contact with the individual. The imprinting may be based more on the ambience and/or practices of the organization. Higgins, who calls this career imprinting, said "an organizational career imprint is the set of capabilities and connections, coupled with the confidence and cognition that a group of individuals share as a result of their career experiences at a common employer during a particular period in time."[2] Whether the imprint is individual or organizational, the knowledge transferred/learned helps to build LSI. Having seen and or/experienced what works and what does not work, a leader has a broader and more refined repertoire of responses and possible solutions to issues/problems and additionally the resource base to contemplate innovative solutions or to create totally new solutions.

A third type of learning opportunity is imprinting via extended training or professional development. This is the type of learning typically associated with those who are lifelong learners or, at least, with those who are in professions that require continuing education for renewal of licenses or certification in latest techniques.

A leader who stops learning and does not progress will almost certainly fail at some point. The changing global environment that reaches into the smallest and most obscure corner of any enterprise will render old knowledge obsolete and the leader with it. Once again proactive seeking of learning opportunities is essential. Find those learning opportunities that have the potential to affect you individually and avail yourself of them.

A final but equally important type of learning is critical self-reflection. Polizzi and Frick state that "critical self-reflection and engagement with the experiences and critical incidents of one's life is essential."[3] McAlpin and Weston shared regarding teachers engaging in reflective practice that "ongoing use of the process of reflection is essential for building knowledge, and increasing knowledge increases one's ability to use reflection effectively and to develop as a teacher."[4] Their statement applies equally well to leaders. Friedman perhaps said it best:

> Becoming a better leader requires constant reflection—making sense of your experience and then discovering ways to use your insights to increase your impact. Then, to stay ever sharp, it's good to teach what you've learned (and then try to teach what you still *want* to learn). Learning leadership by doing it—what's called *action learning*, which is what you've been engaged in through your efforts with this book—is effective only when you take the time to reflect on what worked, what didn't work, and what you might do differently in the future. Looking back is a necessary step in the process of learning and performance improvement in which you've invested much so far. If you give short shrift to the task of reflection, then the lessons don't get internalized. They don't last.[5]

This internalization of learning allows the final step in Maslow's hierarchy of needs, self-actualization. As Maslow said about self-actualization, "What a man *can* be, he *must* be. This need we may call self-actualization."[6] It is by this process that leaders, and followers, gain the greatest insight into their own character, skills, and abilities. Critical reflection is also the means by which a leader develops a vision for an organization and sets about establishing the resources and tasks needed to achieve that vision.

The first three learning opportunities represent the external influence on learning and the reliance on others. And, reliance on others for learning opportunities is the norm. But self-reliance in seeking learning opportunities is also important whether through reflection, seeking mentors, learning via imprinting by being cognizant of opportunities when observing leaders and/ or organizational functioning, or critical self-reflection.

As Turesky and Wood state, "we have concluded that leadership development is a highly individual learning process."[7] And as Korthagen shared about reflective practice, "It is vital that employees learn how to manage their own development, so that they learn from each new experience, and become ever more proficient at independently integrating new insights into their day-to-day activities."[8] Aspiring leaders must be proactive in seeking the knowledge they need to apply the skills they learn.[*]

The resourceful aspiring leader will use all of the types of learning opportunities. He/she will be a lifelong learner and will use what he/she has learned to navigate the leadership challenges he/she will face. The leader will also realize that all elements of LSI interact with each other to produce the characteristics and skills that define them as a leader. This leader will come to have a quite advanced internalized GPS that utilizes these elements to steer a true course to success.

*For a free *LSI assessment,* go to www.LeadershipIntelligencelsi.com.

Chapter 9

'A Rough Road'

Avoiding Leadership Derailment

Ever been traveling down a busy road and encountered a person walking along the side of the road with a gas can in his/her hand? It's hard to believe that even with all of the technological advances, warning lights, dinging bells, and gauges that someone in this day and age could run out of gas. But it happens. When this happens, the 'journey' takes a back seat to the immediate 'derailment.' Sometimes after a short walk to retrieve a full can of gas, the driver is back on the road. For others, it may not be as simple. Perhaps the opportunity to get a fuel refill is quite far away. Worse yet, something more could complicate the initial trip to 'fill the can.'

In spite of the capabilities of an updated GPS, it cannot force the driver to stop and get gas. Only the driver has the capacity to make that determination. Neither can the automobile choose to do so on its own. The only way for a successful *true north* journey is with an astute driver.

Chapter 3 contained a brief discussion dealing with leadership failure as it relates to credibility. That discussion focused on three categories of leaders who fail: those who commit unlawful acts; those who commit questionable acts; and those who are derailed. Leaders in the first two categories, with rare exceptions, lose credibility and no longer lead. Those leaders made poor choices and paid the price for those choices. Leaders in the third category, derailed leaders, often find another chance to lead. So, what exactly is derailment?

Derailment, which has been extensively examined in business research, is defined in a variety of ways. For Beaumont, "Derailment is said to have happened when leaders—who may have shown a good record of success and who seem to possess the necessary skills, abilities and knowledge to succeed—suddenly and spectacularly fail."[1] The Center for Creative Leadership shared that

A derailed manager is one who, having reached the general manager level, is fired, demoted, or reaches a career plateau. It's important to note that organizations saw the derailed manager as having high potential for advancement, as having impressive track records, and holding a solidly established leadership position—until they derailed. Derailment doesn't refer to individuals who have topped out in their company's hierarchy or to managers who elect to stay at a particular level.[2]

Van Velsor and Ascalon offer a somewhat similar definition, "A derailed executive is one who, having reached the general manager level, finds that there is little chance of future advancement due to a misfit between job requirements and personal skills. The executive is either plateaued or leaves the organization altogether."[3]

From Burke, "Derailment in a leadership or executive role is defined as being involuntarily plateaued, demoted or fired below the level of expected achievement or reaching that level but unexpectedly failing."[4] Furnham, in his seminal work on leader failure, found:

The work on leaders who fail is marked by a number of different terms. The choice of the terms seem relatively arbitrary and the personal favourite of a writer or of people in a particular discipline. Technically they do have slightly different meanings. The following is an incomplete list from an ever-growing group of words used in this area.

- Aberrant (leaders) This emphasizes abnormality, atypicality and deviance from the right or normal type. It has two themes: both unusualness and also a departure from acceptable standards. That is, it has a statistical *and* moral side to it.
- Anti-social (leaders) This echoes the immoral nature of leaders who can be anti-social in the way selfish people may be, but more likely the way delinquents are anti-social. More importantly, perhaps, it echoes the new term for psychopath: anti-social personality disorder.
- Dark side (Triad) (leaders) This is to contrast the bright and the dark; the outside, the obvious and the straightforward with the inside, the obscure and the devious. Dark implies evil, dismal and menacing. The triad suggests three separable constituents of evil.
- Derailed (leaders) This emphasizes the idea of being thrown off course. Trains on tracks derail. Leaders set fair in a particular direction deviate from the path, unable to move forward. It is sometimes hyphenated with the next word in the dictionary, namely *deranged* which implies not only a breakdown in performance but also insanity.
- Despotic (leaders) This is taken from the historical literature emphasizing the misuse and abuse of power by oppressive, absolutist leaders. It emphasizes the autocratic type or style of leadership.

- Destructive (leaders) Used by historians in this context to look at the impact of a particular leadership style, it speaks of the ruining, spoiling or neutralizing of a group or force led by a particular person.
- Incompetent (leaders) This is used to suggest inadequate, ineffective, unqualified. It implies the absence of something required rather than the presence of something not required. Incompetent leaders are ineffective because they are lacking in particular qualities.
- Malignant (leaders) These are leaders who spread malevolence, the antonym of benevolence. Malevolence is misconduct, doing harm such as maliciously causing pain or damage. Malignant leaders, like cancer, grow fast and are deadly.
- Toxic (leaders) This refers to the poisonous effect leaders have on all they touch. Toxic substances kill rather than repel. Again this refers to the consequences of a particular leadership style.
- Tyrannical (leaders) Tyrants show arbitrary, oppressive and unjust behaviour. Tyrants tend to usurp power and then brutally oppress those they command.[5]

The common theme in these definitions is that an up-and-coming, promising leader at some point is no longer able to lead successfully. The leader has risen through the ranks, paid his/her dues, mastered his/her trade/profession to a point in time, is seen as having leadership potential, and is elevated to a leadership position. Then he or she fails as a leader. But, how does derailment happen?

A range of opinions exist as to the causes of derailment. Hogan related that "We believe failure is more related to having undesirable qualities than lacking desirable ones."[6] Hogan, citing Bentz, "identified seven themes associated with derailment. Briefly, these themes are: (1) unable to delegate or prioritize; (2) being reactive rather than proactive; (3) unable to maintain relationships with an extended network of contacts; (4) unable to build a team; (5) having poor judgment; (6) being a slow learner; and (7) having an overriding personality defect."[7]

Furnham posits that "executive derailment is *a* function of three things; very-particular personality traits, naive followers and particular situations that create poorly regulated and governed businesses." First, the particular personality traits. Researchers in this area now talk of the 'dark triad' of subclinical psychopathy. . . . The three interrelated traits of the 'dark triad' are arrogance, duplicitousness, and emotional coldness. What about the second condition of CEO failure; the naive followers? Some types of people allow derailing leaders to thrive—after all, we get the politicians and leaders we deserve. But there is a type of follower that can be termed 'toxic'. . . . Toxic followers become particularly dangerous when they sit on the boards of companies with a derailing CEO.[8]

With regard to the third element Furnham says, "The third component of executive derailment is the social, economic and legal climate. The toxic leader does best in situations of flux and instability."[9] Furnham also suggests that potential leaders should be screened for 'dark side' as well as 'bright side' characteristics during the hiring process and lists seven characteristics of leaders with derailment potential:

Arrogance—They are right and everybody else is wrong
Melodrama—They want to be the center of attention
Volatility—Their mood swings create business swings
Excessive caution—They can't make important decisions
Habitual distrust—They focus on the negatives all the time
Aloofness—They disengage and disconnect from staff
Eccentricity—They think it is fun to be different just for the sake of it
Passive resistance—Their silence is misinterpreted as agreement
Perfectionism—They get the little things right even if the big things go wrong
Eagerness to please—They stress that being popular matters most.[10]

Van Velsor and Leslie in their review of derailment found that "there are four enduring themes." They are present, both over time and across countries. They include problems with interpersonal relationships; failure to meet business objectives; failure to build and lead a team; and inability to change or adapt during a transition.[11]

In summary, derailment occurs for a variety of reasons, but personality traits such as arrogance or aloofness often play a role while organizational themes such as failure to build a team or to reach established goals may also play a part.

One last question with the regard to derailment and the most important question is, can derailment be avoided? Van Velsor and Leslie answer 'yes,' saying:

> Derailment is a fact of life in organizations. Only a relatively few managers will get beyond general management ranks, either because of a lack of fit for more senior level jobs or the lack of open positions in increasingly leaner organizations. Downsizing has added to the likelihood that even generally competent people will derail.
>
> Derailment can be prevented, but only if managers and those around them are willing to work on some relatively tough developmental issues. Improvement in any of the four areas represented by the derailment themes described in this article requires that managers take an in-depth look at personal issues such as self-efficacy, self-esteem and need for control. Understanding why it may be difficult to relate comfortably to others, to learn in the face of change or to let

go of personal achievement in favor of team-building may involve facing issues around trust, security, self-confidence or power. The learning that is involved can be highly emotional, demanding an elevated level of readiness or maturity on the part of managers.[12]

George holds:

> To stay grounded executives must prepare themselves to confront enormous complexities and pressures. Key concepts include: Leaders who move up have greater freedom to control their destinies, but also experience increased pressure and seduction. Leaders can avoid these pitfalls by devoting themselves to personal development that cultivates their inner compass, or True North. This requires reframing their leadership from being heroes to being servants of the people they lead.[13]

George's comments bring us back to the Leadership GPS model. Only through developing LSI and following an internalized Leadership GPS can you navigate through the obstacles you will surely encounter to reach *your true north* and success as a leader.

Chapter 10

Remember, It's All about the Journey

So we've learned all about Leadership Intelligence (LSI), imprinting, and the Leadership GPS model. Now it's time to try out our wheels traveling about the country. Our GPS maps have been updated, we have uploaded our final destination, and we are buckled in ready to make the trip.

The vision for this trip, including the time to start and the estimated time of arrival, is an important goal. Yet, there is so much more to the trip. Surely, along the route there will be routine stops for the creature comforts, as well as waypoints as part of the bigger picture. And, there are always potential hazards along the way in spite of the very best planning.

Automotive imperfections and even possible medical emergencies may lie ahead and temporarily derail even the most prepared driver. However, the most important thing along this journey is to acknowledge the journey itself for *its* value. This trip, regardless of its direction, is part of *your true north*. Within this trip lies a portion of your life and *your total* travel time, so be sure to make the most of *all of the journey*, not just arriving at the destination.

Likewise, the whole gamut of leadership is not just about the outcomes, though those are certainly important, but what is equally important is the journey. It's not about when you start and when you finish. Leadership opportunities may come early in a profession and others may come late in a profession. Some opportunities may be short-lived, while yet others may last an entire career.

Whether the opportunity comes early or late, is short lived or long term, *the journey is as important as the outcome*. It is about what and how you learned and grew along the way. It is about who you help along the way and who helped you (and did you take the time to thank them)? What were the momentous, defining moments in the journey? Did 'what have you internalized' allow you to succeed? Did you enjoy the journey by taking the time to 'stop and smell the roses' without getting derailed? When you arrived at your destination, were you able to reflect on the journey and acknowledge highlights, accomplishments, and new awarenesses?

Bennis described the leadership journey with an analogy to Shakespeare saying that "Shakespeare, who seems to have learned more every time I read him, spoke of the seven ages of man. A leader's life has seven ages as well, and, in many ways, they parallel those Shakespeare describes in *As You Like It*. To paraphrase, these stages can be described as infant, schoolboy, lover, soldier, general, statesman, and sage."[1]

Bennis is referring to a lifetime of leadership. And leadership is just that, a lifetime journey. The transitions Bennis describes will come to all who seek and ultimately fill leadership positions with the passage of time. Aspiring leaders and especially those with the ambition to excel and/or reach the highest leadership levels in their chosen field seldom have time to dwell on the age, the stage, or the transitional period in their early professional years.

Not until they are near the end of their career do they have time to reflect more deeply. That is not to say that leaders do not reflect on what they do, but simply that they often do not reflect regularly on where they are in their career (though perhaps they should). For only by retrospectively examining what we have said and done, how we have said it or done it, and the outcomes generated by our words and actions, can we truly grow. It is not enough to simply say, 'well that worked' or 'that did not work.'

We must critically examine each step/factor and learn from both our successes and failures. As Polizzi et al. stated, "Reflection plays a structural and foundational part in this process of learning from life experiences, and critical self-reflection is a central component to transformative learning."[2] Reflection is also the basis for seeking the learning experiences that will provide continued growth individually and professionally.

For most leaders, the transition from one stage to the next is either incremental or comes at such pace as to seem to be seamlessly moving from one leadership role or opportunity to the next. And, most leaders do not see quick jumps from one leadership level to the next. The transitions are typically less rapid calling for longer stops along the way.

As Kotter shared, "The requirements for leadership include some things that are very situation-specific and that tend to take time, often much time, to develop."[3] A select few, through serendipity, good timing, or just 'plain old good luck' seem to move through the career stages more rapidly. Kotter observed of these atypical individuals, "All this does not preclude the existence of a few unusually broad and talented people who can move easily across industries and companies. There will always be some people like that. But they will always be rare."[4] Again, we refer back to our reference in chapter 3, of those who are genetically predisposed toward leadership.

The typical leader needs to be a lifelong, reflective learner, one who seeks not only new experiences and but experiences related to daily, routine tasks that broaden and deepen his/her leadership skills. Successful leaders are never too old or so experienced that they cannot benefit from learning.

Each of those career changes is like a 'leg' of a cross-country trip. Each time you traverse familiar territory, you become more adept at traveling through it and each time, less in need of your GPS. You learn the pitfalls to avoid and the shortcuts along the route. Mastering the craft and intricacies of leading a business or school takes time and effort. And, school's leaders, though they share some commonalties with their business counterparts, differ in that the product they deal with, educating humans, differs substantially from the typical product of a business enterprise.

Individual people are a lot more variable than components on an assembly line, the branding of a cleaning product, or the dollar balance on a ledger. But whether leading a business or leading a school, a leader needs the skills to manage the interpersonal aspects of the job.

For some leaders, the realization that these skills are needed to be successful at leading a highly diverse cadre of individuals with diverse wants and needs comes early; for others, it comes later. The discerning leader recognizes the need for a skillset to appropriately deal with the human aspect of the job and wisely seeks it out.

This skillset, the five leader imperatives of the LSI model (*credibility, competence, the ability to inspire, vision, and emotional intelligence*), has been described in the previous chapters. Although having any one of the abilities in the skillset is a plus, none of them individually will create success as a leader. You must at least have a modicum of each of them to be successful and the more you have, the more likely your success will be. Each skill in the skillset offers its own unique challenges for individual growth and collectively pose an even greater challenge.

The challenge in developing credibility is being consistent. The most blatant departures from consistency (or at least that appearance) often appear in the political arena where candidates argue over the minutiae of the voting records or positions on issues. But that is after all politics, positions change as do votes in favor of or against any given proposition. Politicians often, however, pay a price for confirmed inconsistency. They are voted out.

By analogy, the same can be true of all leaders. If a leader fails to live up to the values, he/she espouses by being inconsistent; fails to consistently behave ethically and with integrity; shirks responsibility and is not accountable; or is found to be less than consistently honest, responsible, and sincere. He/she may find that they are turned out or derailed and are unable to lead in their organization. As Baldoni related, it is important that as a leader you should, "Live your values."[5]

Baldoni shared about credibility:

Credibility is a leader's coin of the realm. With it, she can lead people to the Promised Land; without it, she wanders in the desert of lost expectations. Once lost it may be impossible to regain, and so the lesson to any manager who as any aspiration of achieving anything is to guard your credibility and take care you never lose it.[6]

But even if a leader can establish credibility through consistently doing what is right, he/she must still exhibit competence to be effective/successful long term. Any individual (and especially those who are overly ambitious and/or fail to spend the time in place to master their profession) can find themselves 'in over their heads.' That is, they may be capable leaders in general, but lack the level of competence required for the position they hold.

Competence then is a causal necessity for credibility. You cannot be credible without competence. And, competence requires skills not only in the core, hard skills of a profession but in the soft skill areas related to competence delineated in the LSI model: discernibility, perception, conflict resolution skills, problem-solving and decision-making skills, relationship building, planning and implementation, and assessment and evaluation. Lacking core 'hard competencies' in any one of these areas will be problematic in the long term. Skills in these areas must be learned, developed, and continually refined.

If a leader is conscientious in developing and maintaining credibility (and assumes a learning posture that allows him/her to become and remain competent), the probability of being a leader who can inspire others is greatly enhanced. But inspiration (like credibility and competence) must come from a heartfelt genuineness. Those who set out to inspire often find that inspiration is like management of people. Dembowski quotes Quinn as holding that "people don't often need, or respond well to, being managed."[7]

Analogously, people do not often respond well to overt attempts to inspire them. People must see that a leader displays enthusiasm for what he/she does. That he/she is energetic and passionate and that they are optimistic about current and future events in the organization, courageous in their efforts toward building positive outcomes and genuine in what they say and do. A leader who is credible and competent has the basis for inspiration. But other ingredients also play a part.

To truly inspire, a leader must have a vision for an organization. He/she must also be capable of engaging others in both building and implementing that vision. Engagement of organizational members (and having those same organizational members properly implement the organizational vision) requires those same individuals to believe the leader is committed to the organization and the vision, and that he/she has a true sense of direction for implementing the vision, is professional in his/her handling of people and events, is decisive, constantly works toward realization of the vision, and has an eye in all instances toward success today and tomorrow.

These are skills and dispositions that can be learned and honed over time. They are also skills and dispositions that lend themselves to developing a true followership as a leader, not in the sense of a reverent followership, but of people who believe that you will do *what is right*, and do it in the right way because you are about the organization, its members, and the outcomes of the organization.

Guiding the leadership journey of a credible, competent, inspirational leader who has a viable vision that is accepted and acted upon is that leader's emotional intelligence. This is the thread that binds together all of the skills, both hard and soft, and the dispositions of the leader. As Goleman shares, emotionally intelligent leaders are self-aware, self-regulating, motivated, display great empathy toward others, and have highly developed social and interpersonal skills.[8] Such leaders have or develop the skills they need and employ them appropriately when called for. They have a broad and inclusive repertoire of knowledge and skills upon which they can draw on, and have the emotional intelligence to navigate the often challenging roads and byways of leadership.

Consummate leaders display skills and dispositions of the LSI model. One need only examine the leadership shown by those leaders whose GPS's were fully charged and updated. Whether imprinted with LSI by a genetic predisposition, early imprinting (either via stress or desire), the following leaders during their journeys left memorable impressions that will be models for generations of leaders. The charismatic personality and openness of President Ronald Wilson Reagan; the tenacity and genuineness of the Reverend Billy Graham; the relentless and enthusiastic nature of Coach Pat Summit; the tireless compassion of Martin Luther King Jr.; and the idealism and energy of Steve Jobs . . . all leaders in different ways, yet all possessing the skillset to have had hundreds of thousands of willing and enthusiastic followers, even today.

Appendix

Additional Information

CHAPTER 1

How Leadership Imprinting Occurs

Together, the framework suggests that the conceptual domain of imprinting can be organized around five core constructs: *the imprinters, the imprinted,* and the *imprinting processes* that collectively constitute the genesis of imprints, the subsequent evolutionary *dynamics* (path, duration, and evolution of imprints) that contribute to the metamorphosis of imprints, and the *impact of imprints* that become manifest to varying degrees in various outcomes (the outcomes and implications that follow from imprints). Interrelating these constructs, the framework emphasizes fundamental distinctions in the formation, development/dynamics, and consequences of imprinting.

We would, however, hasten to add that there are likely interdependencies and interactions across the phases. Interdependencies occur because the process by which imprints form may shape the subsequent evolution of imprints. Similarly, the nature and evolution of imprints affect the magnitude, timing, and direction of their outcomes. Interactions may also occur between imprinting sources, processes, and dynamics across micro and macro levels of analysis (Marquis and Tilcsik, 2013; Simsek, 2015).

Simsek goes on to suggest that "that imprinting involves three processes in which an imprint is formed (*genesis*), evolves and morphs (*metamorphosis*), and eventually becomes manifest in outcomes (*manifestations*)." He expands those concepts in relating that imprinting involves "*imprinters, imprinted, imprinting, imprint dynamics*, and *impact of imprints*" (Simsek, 2015). The key underlying mechanism is that, during periods of organizational and professional socialization, "individuals are particularly susceptible to influence . . . because of the great uncertainty regarding role requirements" (Ashforth and Saks, 1996: 149).

Because individuals are highly motivated to reduce such uncertainty, they become especially receptive to cues from the environment (Schein, 1971). Thus the first exposure to the practical aspects of a job or position is often highly formative. With limited prior experience in the position, people are not only more open to learning new skills but also "more receptive to learning . . . work routines and practices" (Briscoe and Kellogg, 2011: 295). Later, by contrast, people tend to be "less receptive to learning and, therefore, are not susceptible to imprinting" (McEvily, Jaffee, and Tortoriello, 2012: 552; Tilscik, 2014).

Stress Imprints, Desired Imprints, and Mentoring

The key underlying mechanism is that, during periods of organizational and professional socialization, "individuals are particularly susceptible to influence . . . because of the great uncertainty regarding role requirements" (Ashforth and Saks, 1996: 149). Because individuals are highly motivated to reduce such uncertainty, they become especially receptive to cues from the environment (Schein, 1971).

Thus, the first exposure to the practical aspects of a job or position is often highly formative. With limited prior experience in the position, people are not only more open to learning new skills but also "more receptive to learning . . . work routines and practices" (Briscoe and Kellogg, 2011: 295).

REFERENCES

Marquis, Christopher and András Tilcsik. "Imprinting: Toward a Multilevel Theory." *The Academy of Management Annals* 7, no. 1 (2013): 195–245.

Zeki, Simsek, Brian Fox, and Ciaran Heavey. "What's Past Is Prologue: Framework, Review, and Future Directions for Organizational Research on Imprinting." *Journal of Management* 41, no. 1 (January 2015): 288–317.

Ashforth, Blake K., and Alan M. Saks. "Socialization Tactics: Longitudinal Effects on Newcomer Adjustment." *Academy of Management Journal* 39, no. 1 (1996): 149–178.

Schein, E. H. "The Individual, the Organization, and the Career: A Conceptual Scheme." *Journal of Applied Behavioral Science* 7, no. 4 (1971): 401–426.

Briscoe, F., and K. C. Kellogg. "The Initial Assignment Effect: Local Employer Practices and Positive Career Outcomes for Work-Family Program Users." *American Sociological Review* 76, no. 2 (2011): 291–319.

McEvily, B., Jaffee, J., and Tortoriello, M. "Not All Bridging Ties Are Equal: Network Imprinting and Firm Growth in the Nashville Legal Industry, 1933–1978." *Organization Science* 23, no. 2 (2011): 547–563.

Notes

PREFACE

1. Daniel Goleman, "What Makes a Leader?" In *HBR's 10 Must Reads on Emotional Intelligence* (Boston, MA: Harvard Business Press, 2015), 7.

INTRODUCTION

1. Allison King, "Former Mayor Tom Menino Recalls Boston Marathon Bombing, Manhunt," *NECN,* 2014, www.necn.com/news/newengland/Former-Mayor-Tom-Menino-Recalls-Boston-Marathon-Bombing-Manhunt-281003832.html.
2. Tom Brokaw, *The Greatest Generation* (New York: Random House, 1998).

CHAPTER 1

1. Benjamin Bloom, "New Views of the Learner: Implications for Instruction and Curriculum" (Educational Leadership, 1978), 563–579.
2. Daniel Goleman, "What Makes a Leader?" In *HBR's 10 Must Reads on Emotional Intelligence* (Boston, MA: Harvard Business Press, 2015), 7.
3. Daniel Goleman, Richard Boyatzis, and Annie McKee, *Primal Leadership* (Boston, MA: Harvard Business Press, 2010).
4. Goleman, "What Makes a Leader?"
5. GMAC.com/market-intelligence-and-research/research-library/curriculum-insight/2014-gmegs-survey-report.aspx.
6. Bloom, "New Views of the Learner."
7. Howard Gardner, *Frames of Mind: The Theory of Multiple Intelligences* (New York, NY: Basic Books).

8. Klaus Immelmann, "Ecological Significance of Imprinting and Early Learning." *Annual Review of Ecology and Systematics*, Vol. 6 (1975): 15–37.

9. Branti Film Productions (Producers). Carroll Ballard. (Director). *Fly Away Home*. United States, Columbia Pictures (1996).

10. Bill Lishman, *Father Goose* (Little Brown: Toronto, ON, 1995).

11. Robert Miller, *Imprint Training of the Newborn Foal* (Morris Communications Corporation: Augusta, GA, 2003).

12. Christopher Marquis and Andras Tilscik, *Imprinting: Toward a Multilevel Theory. Academy of Management Annals* (Routledge: New York, 2013).

13. Ibid.

14. Arthur Stinchcombe, "Social Structure and Organizations." In J. G. March, *Handbook of Organizations* (Rand McNally: Chicago, IL, 1965).

15. Pete Hall, "Building Bridges: Strengthening the Principal Induction Process through Intentional Mentoring." *Phi Delta Kappan*, Vol. 89, Issue 6 (2008): 449–452.

16. James M. Kouzes and Barry Z. Posner, "Challenge Is the Opportunity for Greatness." *Leader to Leader*, Vol. 2003, Issue 28 (2003): 16–23.

17. Marquis and Tilcsik, *Imprinting: Toward a Multilevel Theory*.

18. Ibid.

19. Monica Higgins, *Career Imprints: Creating Leaders Across an Industry*. First edition (San Francisco, CA: Jossey-Bass, 2005).

20. Marquis and Tilcsik, *Imprinting: Toward a Multilevel Theory*.

21. Zeki Simsek, Brian Fox, and Ciaran Heavey, "What's Past Is Prologue: Framework, Review, and Future Directions for Organizational Research on Imprinting." *Journal of Management*, Vol. 41, Issue 1 (January 2015): 288–317.

22. Ibid.

23. Marquis and Tilcsik, 2013; Simsek, 2015.

24. See appendix for further reading.

25. Marquis and Tilcsik, *Imprinting: Toward a Multilevel Theory*.

26. Ibid. See appendix for further reading.

CHAPTER 2

1. Bill George and Peter Sims, *True North: Discover Your Authentic Leadership* (San Francisco, CA: Jossey-Bass, 2007).

2. Ibid.

3. Ibid.

4. Ibid.

5. Jim Collins, *Good to Great* (HarperCollins Publishers, Inc., 2001).

CHAPTER 3

1. Salaryforbusiness.com. Cracking the dress code dilemma. Retrieved from: http://business.salary.com/cracking-the-dress-code-dilemma/ (2015).

2. Lou Solomon, "The Top Complaints from Employees About Their Leaders." *Harvard Business Review*. Retrieved from: https://hbr.org/2015/06/the-top-complaints-from-employees-about-their-leaders.

3. James Kouzes and Barry Pozner, *Credibility: How Leaders Gain and Lose it, Why People Demand It* (San Francisco, CA: Jossey-Bass, 2011).

4. Brian Leavy, "Understanding the Triad of Great Leadership—Context, Conviction, and Credibility." *Strategy and Leadership,* Vol. 31, Issue 1 (2003): 56.

5. Brenda DePuy, "The Linchpins of Leadership." *Public Manager*, Vol. 44, Issue 2 (2015): 6–8.

6. Stephen R. Covey, "Unifying Leadership." *Executive Excellence*, Vol. 16, Issue 10 (1999): 3.

7. Ken Blanchard, *The Secret: What Great Leaders Know and Do* (San Francisco, CA: Berrett-Koeher Publishers, Inc., 2001).

8. https://en.wikipedia.org/wiki/Walter_Cronkite.

9. Prasad Kaipa, "Recover Your Credibility." Retrieved from: https://hbr.org/2012/.

10. DePuy, "The Linchpins of Leadership."

11. James Kouzes, *T + D*, Vol. 64, Issue 9 (2010): 70–71.

12. Bob Pockrass. "Dale Earnhardt Jr. May Have to Win Back Fans' Trust after Laying Back." *Sporting News*, May 5, 2014. Retrieved from: http://www.sportingnews.com/nascar-news/4582977-dale-earnhardt-jr-strategy-talladega-finish-results-fan-reaction-tweets/.

13. Krysten Crawford, Martha Stewart Inks TV Deal. *CNN Money*. Retrieved from: http://money.cnn.com/2004/12/08/news/newsmakers/martha_tv/index.htm.

14. A. Axelrod, *Patton: A Biography* (New York: Palgrave Macmillan, 2006).

15. Greg Botelho, Matt Smith, and Ashley Fantz, NBA Commissioner Bans Clippers Owner Sterling, Pushes to 'Force a Sale' of Team. *CNN*. Retrieved from: http://www.cnn.com/2014/04/29/us/clippers-sterling-scandal/index.html.

16. Kayla Webley, "Hey, Hey, Hey, Goodbye: Mark Hurd, Hewlett-Packard." *TIME*. Retrieved from: http//content.time.com/time/specials/packages/article/0,28804,2009445 _ 2009441,00.html (2010).

17. Peter Drucker. "What Makes an Effective Executive?" *Harvard Business Review*, Vol. 82, Issue 6 (2004): 58–63.

18. *Marked by Teachers.com*, "Billy Graham Was a Role Model." Retrieved from: http://www.markedbyteachers.com/gcse/religious-studies-philosophy-and-ethics/billy-graham-was-a-role-model.html.

19. Aren Langvardt, "Ethical Leadership and the Dual Roles of Examples." In *CIBER Special Issue: Business Ethics & Intellectual Property in the Global Marketplace* (2012).

20. Linda Galindo, "The Power of Accountability." *Leader to Leader*, Vol. 10, Issue 56 (2010): 17–20.

21. James Kouzes and Barry Posner, "To Lead, Create a Shared Vision." *Harvard Business Review*, Vol. 87, Issue 1 (2009): 20–21.

22. James O'Toole and Warren Bennis, "What's Needed Next: A Culture of Candor?" *Harvard Business Review*, Vol. 87, Issue 6 (2009): 54–61.

23. Ibid.

24. Ibid.

25. Galindo, "The Power of Accountability."

26. Mathews Mitford, *A Dictionary of Americanisms on Historical Principles* (Chicago: University of Chicago Press, I). Retrieved from: http:// www.trumanlibrary.org/buckstop.htm (1951).

27. *The Pat Summitt Foundation*; patsummitt.org

28. Ibid.

29. Galindo. "The Power of Accountability."

30. Warren Bennis. *On Becoming a Leader* (New York: Basic Books, 2003).

31. Ibid.

32. David Mineo, "The Importance of Trust in Leadership." *Research Management Review*, Vol. 20, Issue 1 (2014).

33. Warren Bennis, *On Becoming a Leader.*

34. Carly Fiorina, *Tough Choices: A Memoir* (New York: Portfolio, 2006).

35. Donna E. Shalala, "The Buck Starts Here." *Public Integrity*, Vol. 6, Issue 4 (2004): 349–356.

36. Ibid.

37. Marked by Teachers.com, "Billy Graham was a Role Model."

38. Tessa Bashford, Lynn Offerman, and Tara Behrend, "Please Accept my Sincerest Apologies: Examining Follower Reactions to Leader Apology." *Journal of Business Ethics*, Vol. 119, Issue 1 (2014): 99–117.

39. Ibid.

CHAPTER 4

1. http://www.thefamouspeople.com/profiles/sam-walton-209.php.

2. Lee G. Bolman, and Terrance E. Deal, *Reframing Organizations: Artistry, Choice, and Leadership.* Fourth Edition (San Francisco, CA: Jossey-Bass, 2015).

3. Jeff Boss, "The Leadership Guide to Choosing the Right Words." *Forbes.* Retrieved from: http://www.forbes.com/sites/jeffboss/2015/10/02/the-leadership-guide-to-choosing-the-right-words/.

4. Contemporary English Version of the King James Bible. I Kings 3:16-28.

5. Christopher Day and David Gurr, *Leading Schools Successfully: Stories from the Field* (London: Routledge, 2014), 194–208.

6. Peter Drucker, "What Makes an Effective Executive?" *Harvard Business Review*, Vol. 82, Issue 6 (2004): 58–63.

7. Bolman and Deal, *Reframing Organizations: Artistry, Choice and Leadership.*

8. Ibid.

9. http://www.mediate.com/articles/ebarker4.cfm.

10. Stephen Covey, *The Seven Habits of Highly Effective People* (New York: Free Press, 1989).

11. Ibid.

12. http://www.history.com/this-day-in-history/stock-market-crashes.

13. Robert Tannenbaum and Warren Schmidt, "How to Choose a Leadership Pattern." *Harvard Business Review*, Vol. 51, Issue 3 (1973): 162–180.

14. Dennis Reina and Michelle Reina, *Trust and Betrayal in the Workplace: Building Effective Relationships in your Organization* (San Francisco, CA: Berrett-Koehler, 1999).

15. Ibid.

16. http://brandmakernews.com/personal-brand/3116/making-connections-the-bill-clinton-way-2.html#sthash.IIRXZ4sl.dpuf.

17. Reina and Reina, *Trust and Betrayal in the Workplace: Building Effective Relationships in your Organization.*

18. Marshall Goldsmith, "How Not to Lose the Top Job." *Harvard Business Review*, Vol. 87, Issue 1 (2009): 72–80.

CHAPTER 5

1. United States Department of Defense. *GPS Spectrum and Interference Issues.* Retrieved from: http://www.gps.gov/spectrum/ (2012).

2. John Baldoni, "Use Your Leadership Presence to Inspire." *Harvard Business Review.* Retrieved from: https://hbr.org/2010/05/use-your-leadership-presence-to-inspire (2010).

3. Peter F. Drucker, "What Makes an Effective Executive?" *Harvard Business Review*, Vol. 82, Issue 6 (2004): 58–63.

4. Baldoni, "Use Your Leadership Presence to Inspire."

5. http://www.thefamouspeople.com/profiles/martin-luther-king-jr-48.php.

6. John Baldoni, "Wanted: Inspirational Leaders." *Conference Board Review*, Vol. 46, Issue 4 (2009): 6–7.

7. Meena S. Wilson and Susan S. Rice, "Wired to Inspire: Leading Organizations Through Adversity." *Leadership in Action*, Vol. 24, Issue 2 (May 2004): 3–7.

8. Dov Seidman, "Catalyzing Inspirational Leadership: Approaches and Metrics for Twenty-First-Century Executives." *Leader to Leader*, Vol. 2, Issue 68 (2013): 33–40.

9. https://en.wikipedia.org/wiki/Christa_McAuliffe.

10. Jack Zenger and Joseph Folkman, "I'm the Boss! Why Should I Care If You Like Me." *Harvard Business Review* (2013).

11. Myron Glassman and R. Bruce, McAfee, "Enthusiasm: The Missing Link in Leadership." *SAM Advanced Management Journal* (07497075), Vol. 55, Issue 3 (1990): 4.

12. Jill Frymier Russell, "Enthusiastic Educational Leadership." *Florida Journal of Educational Administration & Policy*, Vol. 1, Issue 2 (2008): 79–97.

13. Jennifer M. George, "Emotions and Leadership: The Role of Emotional Intelligence." *Human Relations*, Vol. 53, Issue 8 (2000): 1027–1055.

14. Ibid.

15. Russell, "Enthusiastic Educational Leadership."

16. Jerry L. Patterson and Paul Kelleher, *Resilient School Leaders: Strategies for Turning Adversity into Achievement*, Association for Supervision & Curriculum Development (ASCD). Alexandria, VA: USA (2005).

17. Jim Loehr and Tony Schwartz, *The Power of Full Engagement: Managing Energy, not Time, is the Key to High Performance and Personal Renewal* (New York: Free Press, 2003).

18. Patterson and Kelleher, *Resilient School Leaders: Strategies for Turning Adversity into Achievement.*

19. John Coleman, Daniel Gulati, and W. Oliver Segovia, "Passion and Purpose: Stories from the Best and Brightest Young Business Leaders." (n.d.).

20. Alaina Love, "Leadership, Passion, and the Presidency." *Harvard Business Review*. Retrieved from: https://hbr.org/2008/10/leadership-passion-and-the-presidency/ (2008).

21. Alaina Love, "Passion and Purpose: Leading from the Inside Out." *Leader to Leader*, Vol. 65 (2012): 50–56. Doi:10.1002/ltl.20036.

22. Ibid.

23. Brent Davies and Tim Brighouse, "Management in Education." *British Educational Leadership, Management and Administration Society (BELMAS)*, Vol. 24, Issue 1 (2010): 4–6.

24. Ibid.

25. http://www.forbes.com/sites/carminegallo/2012/08/08/5-reasons-why-optimists-make-better-leaders/.

26. Liz Wiseman, "Your Optimism Might Be Stifling Your Team." *Harvard Business Review*. Retrieved from: https://hbr.org/2013/05/your-optimism-might-be-stifling-your-team (2013).

27. Justin Menkes, "Maintaining Clarity of Thought: Leading Better Under Pressure." *Leader to Leader*, Vol. 62 (2011): 22–26, Doi: 10.1002/ltl.488.

28. http://www.forbes.com/sites/carminegallo/2012/08/08/5-reasons-why-optimists-make-better-leaders/.

29. Donovan A. McFarlane, "Impressed and Inspired: Encountering Genuine Leadership with Dr. Barry Posner and Dr. Agueda Ogazon." *E Journal of Organizational Learning & Leadership*, Vol. 9, Issue 1 (2011): 26–48.

30. Rob Goffee and Gareth Jones, "Managing Authenticity." *Harvard Business Review*, Vol. 83, Issue 12 (2005): 86–94.

31. Deborah Gruenfield and Lauren Zander, "Authentic Leadership Can Be Bad Leadership." *Harvard Business Review*. Retrieved from: https://hbr.org/2011/02/authentic-leadership-can-be-bad-leadership/.

32. M. Warrell, "Five Ways to Unlock Authentic Leadership." *Leadership Excellence Essentials*, Vol. 30, Issue 10 (2013): 7.

33. Gruenfield and Zander, "Authentic Leadership Can Be Bad Leadership."

34. Kathleen K. Reardon, "Courage as a Skill." *Harvard Business Review*. Retrieved from: https://hbr.org/2007/01/courage-as-a-skill/ (2007).

35. Ibid.

36. Ford Walston, "Courageous Leadership." *Personal Excellence Essentials*, Vol. 19, Issue 10 (2014): 29–30.

CHAPTER 6

1. Burt Nanus, "Leading The Vision Team." *The Futurist*, Vol. 30, Issue 3 (1996): 20.

2. James Collins and Jerry Porras, "Building Your Company's Vision." *Harvard Business Review*, Vol. 74, Issue 5 (1996): 65–77.

3. Ibid.

4. Warren Bennis, "The Seven Ages of the Leader." *Harvard Business Review*, Vol. 82, Issue 1 (2004): 46–53.

5. Ibid.

6. Ibid.

7. James Kouzes and Barry Posner, "To Lead, Create a Shared Vision." *Harvard Business Review*, Vol. 87, Issue 1 (2009): 20–21.

8. John Kotter, "What Leaders Really Do?" *Harvard Business Review*, Vol. 68, Issue 3 (1990): 103–111.

9. Ibid.

10. John Kotter, "Leading Change: Why Transformation Efforts Fail." *Harvard Business Review*, Vol. 73, Issue 2 (1995): 59–67.

11. Daniel Goleman, "Leading for the Long Future." *Leader to Leader*, Vol. 2014, Issue 72 (2014): 34–39.

12. Ibid.

13. Stephen Covey, "Four Traits of Great Leaders." *Leadership Excellence Essentials*, Vol. 22, Issue 11 (2005): 4–5.

14. Kouzes and Posner, "To Lead, Create a Shared Vision."

15. Ibid.

16. Burt Nanus, *Visionary Leadership: Creating a Compelling Sense of Direction for Your Organization* (San Francisco, CA: Jossey-Bass, 1992).

17. Joseph Murphy and Daniela Torre, "Vision: Essential Scaffolding." *Educational Management Administration & Leadership*, Vol. 43, Issue 2 (2015): 177–197.

18. Sylvia Méndez-Morse, "Vision, Leadership, and Change." SEDL. *Issues . . . about Change*, Vol. 2, Issue 3 (1993). Retrieved from: http://www.sedl.org/change/issues/issues23.html.

19. Ibid.

20. For additional information, visit http://www.sedl.org/change/issues/issues23.html.

21. Mary Crossan, Jeffrey Gandz, and Gerard Seijts, "Developing Leadership Character." *Ivey Business Journal*, Vol. 76, Issue 1 (2012): 3–8.

22. Nanus, *Leading the Vision Team.*

23. James Sarros, Brian Cooper, Joseph Santora, "The Character of Leadership." *Ivey Business Journal*, Vol. 71, Issue 5 (2007): 1.

24. Johannes Steyrer, Michael Schiffinger, Reinhart Lang, "Organizational Commitment – A Missing Link Between Leadership Behavior and Organizational Performance?" *Scandinavian Journal of Management*, Vol. 24, Issue 4 (2008): 364–374.

25. Ibid.

26. GLOBE is a research program focusing on culture and leadership in 61 nations. National cultures are examined in terms of nine dimensions: performance orientation, assertiveness, power distance, humane orientation, institutional collectivism, in-group collectivism, uncertainty avoidance, and gender egalitarianism. In a survey of thousands of middle managers in food processing, finance, and telecommunications industries in these countries, GLOBE compares their cultures and attributes of effective leadership. (Leadership Effectiveness and Culture: The Globe Study. Retrieved from: http://www.ccl.org/leadership/pdf/assessments/globestudy.pdf).

27. Read more at http://www.thefamouspeople.com/profiles/f-d-roosevelt-70. Php#h 15 tYulDGMhbcBVS.

28. John Hamm, "The Five Messages Leaders Must Manage." *Harvard Business Review*, Vol. 84, Issue 5 (May 2006): 115–23. Harvard Business School. MBA Oath; Retrieved from: http://mbaoath.org/wp-content/uploads/2009/05/mba-oath2. pdf (2006).

29. Michael Feiner, "Commitment." *Leadership Excellence Essentials*, Vol. 24, Issue 3 (2007): 12.

30. Gary Yukl and Richard Lepsinger, "Getting It Done: Four Ways to Translate Strategy into Results." *Leadership in Action*, Vol. 27, Issue 2 (2007): 3–7.

31. Karl Walinskas, "From Vision to Reality." *Industrial Management*, Vol. 42, Issue 6 (2000): 22.

32. Daniel Jensen, "Executing the Strategic Plan: Five Actions Midlevel Leaders Can Take." *MWorld*, Vol. 13, Issue 3 (2014): 28–30.

33. Torun Dewan and David P. Myatt, "The Qualities of Leadership: Direction, Communication, and Obfuscation." *American Political Science Review*, Vol. 102, Issue 3 (2008): 351–368.

34. Nanus, *Visionary Leadership: Creating a Compelling Sense of Direction for Your Organization.*

35. Ibid.

36. https://en.wikipedia.org/wiki/David_Packard.

37. Google Code of Conduct. (2015). Retrieved from: https://investor. google. com/corporate/google-code-of-conduct.html - https://investor.google.com/corporate/google-code-of-conduct.html.

38. Ford Corporation. (2015). Code of Conduct Handbook Corporate Policies and Directives. Retrieved from: http://corporate.ford.com/ microsites/sustainability-report-2014–15/doc/sr14-company-governance-corporate-conduct-standards. pdf, http://corporate.ford.com/microsites/sustainability-report-2014–15/doc/sr14-company-governance-corporate-conduct-standards.pdf.

39. J. P. Morgan Chase and Co. (2015). Code of Conduct and Code of Ethics for Finance Professional (Document). https://www.jpmorganchase.com/ corporate/About-JPMC/document/ code-of-conduct.pdf - Online Statement https://www.jpmorganchase.com/corporate/About-JPMC/ab-code-of-ethics.htm.

40. Max Anderson, "Why We Created the MBA Oath." *Harvard Business Review*. Retrieved from: https://hbr.org/2009/06/why-we-created-the-mba-oath/ (2009).

41. AMA. (2015). Medical Ethics. Retrieved from: http://www.ama. assn.org/ ama/pub/physician-resources/medical-ethics.page; Online statement retrieved from: http://www.ama-assn.org/ama/pub/physician-resources/medical-ethics/code-medical-ethics.page.

42. Arizona State Bar Association. (2015). A Lawyer's Creed of Professionalism of the State Bar of Arizona. Retrieved from: http://www.azbar.org/membership/admissions/lawyerscreedofprofessionalism.

43. National Society of Professional Engineers (NSPE) Code of Ethics for Engineers. (2015). Retrieved from: http://www.onlineethics.org/Resources/ethcodes/EnglishCodes/9972.aspx.

44. National Policy Board for Educational Administration. Professional Standards for Educational Leaders. (2015). Reston, VA. Retrieved from: http://www.ccsso.org/ documents/2015/ professionalstandardsforeducationalleaders2015fornpbeafinal.pdf. - ELCC standards - http://www.npbea.org/NCATEELCC.

45. Oregon Standards for Professional Practice. (2015). Oregon State Department of Education. Retrieved from: http://www.ode.state.or.us/ search/page/?id=3768.

46. Daniel Yergin and Joseph Stanislaw, *Commanding Heights* (New York: Simon & Schuster, Inc., 1998).

47. Nick Tasler, "Just Make a Decision Already." *Harvard Business Review.* Retrieved from: https://hbr.org/2013/10/just-make-a-decision-already/ (2013).

48. Ibid.

49. Michael Useem, "Decision Making as Leadership Foundation." *Handbook of Leadership Theory and Practice* (Boston, MA: Harvard Business Press, 2010), 507–526.

50. Ronald A. Howard and Clinton D. Korver, *Ethics for the Real World* (Boston, MA: Harvard Business Press, 2008). Retrieved from: http://common.books24x7.com. lynx.lib.usm.edu/toc.aspx?bookid=27127 (Accessed August 24, 2016).

51. Ibid.

52. Peter Drucker, "The Effective Executive." *Harvard Business Review*. Retrieved from: https://hbr.org/1967/01/the-effective-decision (1967).

53. Ibid.

54. Larry Neal and Carl Spetzler, "An Organization-Wide Approach to Good Decision Making." *Harvard Business Review*. Retrieved from: https://hbr.org/2015/05/ an-organization-wide-approach-to-good-decision-making (2015).

55. Nanus, *Visionary Leadership: Creating a Compelling Sense of Direction for Your Organization.*

56. http://demoss.com/newsrooms/bgea/background/profile-billy-graham.

57. Ian Woodward, "Understanding Values for Insightfully Aware Leadership." *INSEAD Working Papers Collection.*, Issue 46 (2014): 1–58.

58. Ibid.

59. Ibid.

60. Ibid.

61. Alan H. Church, "Managerial Behaviors and Work Group Climate as Predictors of Employee Outcomes." *Human Resource Development Quarterly*, Vol. 6, Issue 2 (1995): 173–205.

62. John P. Meriac, Amanda L. E. Thomas, and Matthew Milunski, "Work Ethic as a Predictor of Task Persistence and Intensity." *Learning & Individual Differences*, Vol. 37 (2015): 249–254.

63. http://www.nytimes.com/2013/06/02/books/review/sum-it-up-by-pat-summitt-with-sally-jenkins.html.

64. Henry Doss, "Five Character Traits of Innovation Leaders." Retrieved from: http://www.forbes.com/sites/henrydoss/2015/09/16/five-character-traits-of-innovation-leaders/ (2015).

65. http://www.thefamouspeople.com/profiles/golda-meir-1532.php.

66. Peter Drucker, "What Makes an Effective Executive." *Harvard Business Review*, Vol. 82, Issue 6 (2004): 58–63.

67. Bennis, "The Seven Ages of the Leader."

68. Jay Conger and Robert Fulmer, "Developing Your Leadership Pipeline." *Harvard Business Review*, Vol. 81, Issue 12 (December 2003): 76–84.

69. J. L. Bower, "Solve the Succession Crises by Growing Inside-Outside Leaders." *Harvard Business Review*, Vol. 85, Issue 11 (2007): 90–96.

CHAPTER 7

1. Daniel Goleman, "What Makes a Leader?" *Harvard Business Review*, Vol. 76, Issue 6 (1998): 93–102.

2. Diane Contu, "How Resilience Works." *Harvard Business Review*. Retrieved from: https://hbr.org/2002/05/how-resilience-works (2002).

3. Joshua Margolis and Paul Stoltz, "How to Bounce Back from Adversity." *Harvard Business Review*. Retrieved from: https://hbr.org/2010/01/how-to-bounce-back-from-adversity (2010).

4. Martin Seligman, "Building Resilience." *Harvard Business Review*. Retrieved from: https://hbr.org/2011/04/building-resilience (2011).

5. Sarah Bond and Gillian Shapiro, "Tough at the Top? The New Rules of Resilience for Women's Leadership Success." Retrieved from: https://forbusinessake.files.wordpress.com/ 2014/11/tough_at_the_top.pdf (2014).

6. Resilience. American Psychological Association. Retrieved from: http://www.apa.org/ helpcenter/road-resilience.aspx (2015).

7. Paul Stoltz, "When Adversity Strikes, What Do You Do?" *Harvard Business Review*. Retrieved from: https//hbr.org/2010/07/when-adversity-strikes-what-do-you-do (2010).

8. Robert Thomas, *Crucibles of Leadership: How to Learn from Experience to Become a Great Leader* (Boston, MA: Harvard Business School Publishing Corporation, 2008).

9. http://www.thefamouspeople.com/profiles/walter-elias-disney-3151.php.

10. Diane Contu, "How Resilience Works." *Harvard Business Review*. Retrieved from: https://hbr.org/2002/05/how-resilience-works/ (2002).

11. APA. "Resilience."

12. Goleman (1998).

13. Ibid.

14. Ibid.

15. Ibid.

16. For more information on building resilience, visit https://hbr.org/2011/04/resilience-for-the-rest-of-us/.

17. Joshua Margolis and Paul Stoltz, "How to Bounce Back from Adversity." *Harvard Business Review*. Retrieved from: https://hbr.org/2010/01/how-to-bounce-back-from-adversity (2010).

18. Ibid.

19. Martin Seligman, "Building Resilience." *Harvard Business Review*. Retrieved from: https://hbr.org/2011/04/building-resilience (2011).

20. http://www.achievement.org/autodoc/page/win0bio-1.

21. Contu, "How Resilience Works."

22. Bond and Shapiro, "Tough At the Top? The New Rules of Resilience for Women's Leadership Success."

23. Eduardo de Oliveira Teixeira and William B. Werther, "Resilience: Continuous Renewal of Competitive Advantages." *Business Horizons*, Vol. 56, Issue 3 (2013): 333–342.

24. Ibid.

25. George Everly, Jr. "Building a Resilient Organizational Culture." *Harvard Business Review.* Retrieved from: https://hbr.org/2011/06/building-a-resilient-organizat.

26. Ibid.

27. For additional reading, visit https://hbr.org/2011/06/building-a-resilient-organizat.

28. Daniel Goleman, "Leadership that Gets Results." *Harvard Business Review*, Vol. 78, Issue 2 (2000): 78–90.

29. John Baldoni, "New Study: How Communication Drives Performance." *Harvard Business Review.* Retrieved from: https://hbr.org/2009/11/new-study-how-communication-drives-performance (2009).

30. John Keyser, "Active Listening Leads to Business Success." *T+D*, Vol. 67, Issue 7 (2013): 26.

31. Boris Gorysberg and Michael Slind, "The Silent Killer of Big Companies." *Harvard Business Review* (2012).

32. Rick Bommelje, "Listening Pays!" *Leader To Leader*, Vol. 2013, Issue 70 (2013): 18–25.

33. Ibid.

34. Bernard T. Ferrari, "The Executive's Guide to Better Listening." *McKinsey Quarterly*, Vol. 2 (2012): 50–65; Arthur W. Hafner (2001). *Pareto's Principle: The 80–20 Rule.* Retrieved from: http://bsu.edu/libraries/ahafner/awh-th-math-pareto.html.

35. Carol Ann Tomlinson, "Communication That Powers Leadership." *Educational Leadership*, Vol. 72, Issue 7 (2015): 90–91.

36. David Grossman, "10 Ways to Properly Communicate to Staff & Clients." *Agent's Sales Journal*, Vol. 16 (2009).

37. Lou Solomon, "The Top Complaints from Employees About Their Leaders." *Harvard Business Review.* Retrieved from: https:/hbr.org/2015/06/the-top-complaints-from-employees-about-their-leaders/ (2015).

38. Grossman, "Complaints." (2015).

39. Holly Weeks, "The Best Memo You'll Ever Write." *Harvard Management Communication Letter*, Vol. 2, Issue 2 (2005): 3–5.

40. Ibid.

41. http://www.thefamouspeople.com/profiles/f-d-roosevelt-70.php.

42. Ed Diener, "Subjective Well-Being." *Psychological Bulletin*, Vol. 95, Issue 3 (1984): 542–575.

43. Lolly Daskal, "10 Amazing Secrets of Happy and Successful Leaders." Inc. Retrieved from: http://www.inc.com/lolly-daskal/10-secretive-habits-of-happy-leaders.html (2015).

44. Ibid.

45. Ibid.

46. Dana L. Joseph, Lindsay Y. Dhanani, Winny Shen, Bridget C. McHugh, and Mallory McCord, "Is a Happy Leader a Good Leader? A Meta-Analytic Investigation of Leader Trait Affect and Leadership." *The Leadership Quarterly*, Vol. 26 (2015): 558–577.

47. Victoria Visser, Daan van Knippenberg, Gerben A. van Kleef, and Barbara Wisse, "How Leader Displays of Happiness and Sadness Influence Follower Performance: Emotional Contagion and Creative Versus Analytical Performance." *The Leadership Quarterly*, Vol. 24, Issue 1 (2013): 172–188.

48. Gretchen Spreitzer and Christine Porath, "Creating Sustainable Performance." *Harvard Business Review*, Vol. 90, Issue 1 (2012): 92–99.

49. Roger Martin, "The Power of Happiness." *Rotman Management Magazine*. Rotman School of Management. University of Toronto. Retrieved from: https://rogerlmartin.com/docs/default-source/Articles/incentives-governance/rotman_spring_05_power_happiness (2005).

50. Ibid.

51. Ibid.

52. http://www.thefamouspeople.com/profiles/dwight-david-eisenhower-1270.php.

53. Fabio Sala, "Laughing All the Way to the Bank." *Harvard Business Review*. Retrieved from: https://hbr.org/2003/09/laughing-all-the-way-to-the-bank (2003).

54. Bell Leadership Institute, "Bell Leadership Study Finds Humor Gives Leaders the Edge." *Business Wire* (English) (2012).

55. Zeynep Merve Unal, "Influence of Leaders' Humor Styles on the Employees' Job Related Affective Well-Being." *International Journal of Academic Research in Accounting, Finance and Management Sciences*, Vol. 4, Issue 1 (2014): 201–211.

56. Gordon Brooks, "Humor in Leadership: State of the Art in Theory and Practice." Paper presented at the Annual Meeting of the Mid-Western Education Research Association (Chicago, IL). Retrieved from: http://files.eric.ed.gov/ fulltext/ ED417113.pdf (1992).

57. Sala, "Laughing All the Way to the Bank."

58. Bell Leadership Institute, "Bell Leadership Study Finds Humor Gives Leaders the Edge."

59. M. Craumer, "Getting Serious About Workplace Humor." *Harvard Management Communication Letter*, Vol. 5, Issue 7 (2002): 3.

60. Eric Romero and Kevin Cruthirds, "The Use of Humor in the Workplace." *Academy of Management Perspectives*, Vol. 20, Issue 2 (2006): 58–69.

61. Steve Tobak, "Why Leaders Need a Sense of Humor." *CBS News*. Retrieved from: http://www.cbsnews.com/news/why-leaders-need-a-sense-of-humor/ (2012).

62. Craumer, "Getting Serious About Workplace Humor" (2012).

63. John M. Digman, "Personality Structure: Emergence of the Five-Factor model." *Annual Review of Psychology*, Vol. 41, Issue 1 (1990): 417.

64. Robert R. McCrea and Oliver P. John, "An Introduction to the Five-Factor Model and its Applications." *Journal of Personality*, Vol. 60, Issue 2 (1992): 175–215.

65. Ibid.

66. David Bergman, Caroline Lornudd, Lennart Sloberg, and Ulrica Von Thiele Schwarz, "Leader Personality and 360-degree Assessments of Leader Behavior." *Scandinavian Journal of Psychology*, Vol. 55, Issue 4 (2014): 389–397. Doi:10.1111/sjop.12130.

67. Ibid.

68. Hege Kornør and Hilmar Nordvik, "Personality Traits in Leadership Behavior." *Scandinavian Journal of Psychology*, Vol. 45, Issue 1 (2004): 49–54. Doi:10.1111/j.1467–9450.2004.00377.x.

69. Nai-Wen Chi and Ta-Rau Ho, "Understanding When Leader Negative Emotional Expression Enhances Follower Performance: The Moderating Roles of Follower Personality Traits and Perceived Leader Power." *Human Relations*, Vol. 67, Issue 9 (2014): 1051–1072.

70. Karianne Kalshoven, Deanne Den Hartog, and Annbel B. De Hoogh, "Ethical Leader Behavior and Big Five Factors of Personality." *Journal of Business Ethics*, Vol. 100, Issue 920 (2011): 349–366.

71. Kempke Eppler, "The Relationship of Goldberg's Big Five Personality Trait Measures of Mid-Level Leaders at Midwest State-Supported Colleges and Universities to the Cameron and Quinn Competing Values Model." *Dissertation Abstracts International Section A*, Vol. 74 (2014).

72. Birgit Schyns, John Maslyn, and Marc PM van Veldhoven, "Can Some Leaders have a Good Relationship with many Followers? The Role of Personality in the Relationship between Leader-Member Exchange and Span of Control." *Leadership & Organization Development Journal*, Vol. 33, Issue 6 (2012): 594–606.

73. Timothy A. Judge and Joyce E. Bono, "Five-Factor Model of Personality and Transformational Leadership." *Journal of Applied Psychology*, Vol. 85, Issue 5 (2000): 751–765.

74. Gianpaolo Abatecola, Gabriele Mandarelli, and Sara Poggesi, "The Personality Factor: How Top Management Teams Make Decisions. A Literature Review." *Journal of Management & Governance*, Vol. 17, Issue 4 (2013): 1073–1100.

75. Michael Mccoby, "To Win the Respect of Followers, Leaders Need Personality Intelligence." *Ivey Business Journal*, Vol. 72, Issue 3 (2008): 1–7.

76. Ibid.

77. Ibid.

78. Joseph Santora, "Assertiveness and Effective Leadership: Is There a Tipping Point?" *Academy of Management Perspectives*, Vol. 21, Issue 3 (2007): 84–86.

79. Daniel Ames and Francis J. Flynn, "What Breaks a Leader: The Curvilinear Relation between Assertiveness and Leadership." *Journal of Personality and Social Psychology*, Vol. 92 (2007): 307–324.

80. Scott Edinger, "The One Skill All Leaders Should Work On." *Harvard Business Review*. Retrieved from: https://hbr.org/2012/03/the-one-skill-all-leaders-shou/ (2012).

81. For more about "The One Skill All Leaders Should Work On," visit https://hbr.org/2012/03/the-one-skill-all-leaders-shou/.

82. Daniel Ames, "I'll Know What You're Like When I See How You Feel: How and When Affective Displays Influence Behavior-Based Impressions." *Psychological Science (Wiley-Blackwell)*, Vol. 20, Issue 5 (2009): 586–593.

83. Darren J. Good and Garima Sharma, "A Little More Rigidity: Firming the Construct of Leader Flexibility." *Journal of Change Management*, Vol. 10, Issue 2 (2010): 155–174.

84. Gary Yukl, "The Importance, Assessment, and Development of Flexible Leadership." Practitioner Forum Presented at the 23rd Annual Conference of the Society for Industrial-Organizational Psychology. San Francisco, CA (2008).

85. David Aaker and Briance Mascarenhas, "The Need for Strategic Flexibility," *Journal of Business Strategy*, Vol. 5, Issue 2 (1984): 74.

86. Puina Soffer, "On the Notion of Flexibility in Business Processes." Proceedings of the CAiSE (Conference on Advanced Information Systems Engineering). Porto, Portugal (2005).

87. Allan Calarco, "Adaptability: Keys for Success." Center for Creative Leadership. Retrieved from: http://www.ccl.org/ leadership/ pdf/ capabilities/0906ABJ. pdf.

88. John R. Schultz, "Creating a Culture of Empowerment Fosters the Flexibility to Change." *Global Business & Organizational Excellence*, Vol. 34, Issue 1 (2014): 41–50.

89. Saifallah Benjaafar, Thomas Morin, and Joseph Talavage, "The Strategic Value of Flexibility in Sequential Decision Making." *European Journal of Operational Research*, Vol. 82, Issue 3 (1995): 438–457.

90. Scott Behson, "Increase Workplace Flexibility and Boost Performance." *Harvard Business Review*. Retrieved from: https://hbr.org/2014/03/increase-workplace-flexibility-and boost-performance/ (2014).

91. Good and Sharma, "A Little More Rigidity: Firming the Construct of Leader Flexibility."

92. Sean Hannah, Robert L. Woolfolk, and Robert G. Lord, "Leader Self-Structure: A Framework for Positive Leadership." *Journal of Organizational Behavior*, Issue 2 (2009): 269.

93. Daniel Goleman, "Leadership that Gets Results." *Harvard Business Review*, Vol. 78, Issue 2 (2000): 78–90.

94. Ibid.

95. Ibid.

96. Bunyamin Akdemir, Orhan Erdem, and Sedat Polat, "Characteristics of High Performance Organizations." *Suleyman Demirel University Journal of Faculty of Economics & Administrative Sciences*, Vol. 15, Issue 1 (2010): 155–174.

97. Jim Collins, "Level 5 Leadership: The Triumph of Humility and Fierce Resolve. (cover story)." *Harvard Business Review*, Vol. 83, Issue 7/8 (2005): 136–146. *Business Source Complete*, EBSCO*host* (Accessed December 23, 2015).

98. Good and Sharma, "A Little More Rigidity: Firming the Construct of Leader Flexibility."

99. Affective Display. In *Psychological Dictionary*. Retrieved from: http:// psychologydictionary.org/affect-display/ (2014).

100. Lauren Szczurek, Benoit Monin, and James J. Gross, "The Stranger Effect: The Rejection of Affective Deviants." *Psychological Science*, Vol. 23, Issue 10 (2012): 1105–1111.

101. Daniel Goleman, "What Makes a Leader?" *Harvard Business Review*, Vol. 76, Issue 6 (1998): 93–102.

102. http://www.thefamouspeople.com/profiles/ronald-reagan-69.php.

103. Goleman, "What Makes a Leader?" (1998).

104. Earnest J. Wilson III. "Empathy is Still Lacking in the Leaders Who Need It Most." *Harvard Business Review*. Retrieved from: https://hbr.org/2015/09/empathy-is-still-lacking-in-the-leaders-who-need-it-most (2015).

105. Leonardo Badea and Nicolae Alexandru Pana, "The Role of Empathy in Developing the Leader's Emotional Intelligence." *Theoretical and Applied Economics*, Vol. 17, Issue 2 (2010): 69–78.

106. http://www.thefamouspeople.com/profiles/dwight-david-eisenhower-1270.php.

107. Warren Bennis, "Respect and Trust." *Leadership Excellence Essentials*, Vol. 31, Issue 1 (2014): 11.

CHAPTER 8

1. Warren Bennis, "The Seven Ages of the Leader." *Harvard Business Review*, Vol. 82, Issue 1 (2004): 46–53.

2. Mary Higgins, *Career Imprints: Creating Leaders Across an Industry.* First edition (San Francisco, CA: Jossey-Bass, 2005).

3. William Frick, "Transformative Preparation and Professional Development: Authentic Reflective Practice for School Leadership." *Teaching & Learning*, Vol. 26, Issue 1 (2012): 20–34.

4. Lynn McAlpin and Cynthia Weston, "Reflection: Issues Related to Improving Professors' Teaching and Students' Learning." *Instructional Science*, Vol. 28, Issue 5–6 (2000): 363–385.

5. Stewart Friedman, *Total Leadership: Be a Better Leader, Have a Richer Life* (Boston, MA: Harvard University Press, 2014).

6. Abraham Maslow, "A Theory of Human Motivation." *Psychological Review*, Vol. 50 (1943): 37–39.

7. Elizabeth Turesky and Diane Wood, "Kolb's Experiential Learning as a Critical Frame for Reflective Practice." *Academic Leadership*, Vol. 8, Issue 3 (2010).

8. Fred A. J. Korthagen, "The Organization in Balance: Reflection and Intuition as Complementary Processes." *Management Learning*, Vol. 36, Issue 3 (2005): 371–387.

CHAPTER 9

1 Lucy Beaumont, "Derailed Leaders." *Training Journal* (2014): 66–69.

2. Center for Creative Leadership. (2001). "The Bad News: Derailment Happens." Retrieved from: http://www.ccl.org/leadership/pdf/publications/badnewsgoodnews.pdf.

3. Ellen Van Velsor and Evelina Ascalon, "The Role and Impact of Leadership Development in Supporting Ethical Action in Organisations." *Journal of Management Development*, Vol. 27, Issue 2 (2008): 187–195.

4. Ronald Burke, "Why Leaders Fail: Exploring the Dark Side." *International Journal of Manpower*, Vol. 27, Issue 1 (2006): 91–100.

5. Furnham, *The Elephant in the Boardroom*.

6. Robert Hogan and Joyce Hogan, "Assessing Leadership: A View from the Dark Side." *International Journal of Selection & Assessment*, Vol. 9, Issue 1/2 (2001): 40.

7. Ibid.

8. Adrian Furnham, "When Leaders Lose the Plot." *Management Today* (2010): 62–66.

9. Adrian Furnham, "Bosses Who Go Off the Rails." *Management Today*. Retrieved from: http://www.managementtoday.co.uk/features/1004503/bosses-who-go-off-the-rails/ (2010).

10. Ibid.

11. Ellen Van Velsor and J. B. Leslie, "Why Executives Derail: Perspectives Across Time and Cultures." *Academy of Management Executive*, Vol. 9, Issue 4 (1995): 62–72.

12. Ellen Van Velsor and Evelina Ascalon, "The Role and Impact of Leadership Development in Supporting Ethical Action in Organisations." *Journal of Management Development*, Vol. 27, Issue 2 (2008): 187–195.

13. Bill George, "Why Leaders Lose Their Way." *Harvard Business School Working Knowledge*. Retrieved from: https://hbr.org/2011/06/why-leaders-lose-their-way (2011).

CHAPTER 10

1. Warren Bennis, "The Seven Ages of the Leader." *Harvard Business Review*, Vol. 82, Issue 1 (2004): 46–53.

2. Joseph Polizzi and William Frick, "Transformative Preparation and Professional Development: Authentic Reflective Practice for School Leadership." *Teaching & Learning*, Vol. 26, Issue 1 (2012): 20–34.

3. John Kotter, "The Leadership Factor." *McKinsey Quarterly*, Issue 2 (1988): 71–78.

4. Ibid.

5. John Baldoni, "Leader's Credibility is Golden." *Harvard Business Review*. Retrieved from: https://hbr.org/2008/11/leaders-credibility-is-golden (2008).

6. Ibid.

7. Frederick Dembowski, "The Changing Roles of Leadership and Management in Educational Administration." *National Council of Professor of Educational Administration* (NCPEA). Retrieved from: http://cnx.org/resources/d72229682136f6830b-1c8a5b217517c7/Dembowski.pdf.pdf (2007).

8. Daniel Goleman, "What Makes a Leader?" *Harvard Business Review*, Vol. 76, Issue 6 (1998): 93–102.

About the Authors

Wanda Maulding Green is a leadership faculty member at the University of South Alabama. She has served in leadership roles as a classroom teacher, coach, assistant principal, and principal in K–12 schools, and also as a department chair, associate dean, and dean at the university level.

Ed Leonard is a retired school superintendent. He has done extensive adjunct work in educational leadership for the University of Southern Mississippi and Southeastern Louisiana University, and currently serves as an adjunct instructor of educational leadership for the University of South Alabama.

www.ingramcontent.com/pod-product-compliance
Lightning Source LLC
Chambersburg PA
CBHW021600210326
41599CB00010B/530